Syzygy

LOUISE BAK

Syzygy

LIVRES DC BOOKS

Cover art by J. W. Stewart.
Author photograph by Maylynn Quan.
Illustrations on pages IX and 115 by Winnie Truong
Book designed and typeset by Primeau Barey, Montreal.
Edited by Jason Camlot for the Punchy Writers Series.

Copyright © Louise Bak, 2011.
Legal Deposit, Bibliothèque et Archives nationales du Québec
and the National Library of Canada, 4th trimester, 2010.

Library and Archives Canada Cataloguing in Publication
Bak, Louise, 1972-
Syzygy / Louise Bak.
Poems.
ISBN 978-1-897190-70-8 (bound).
ISBN 978-1-897190-69-2 (pbk.)
I. Title.
PS8553.A3696S89 2011   C811'.54   C2011-902629-5

For our publishing activities, DC Books gratefully acknowledges the financial
support of the Canada Council for the Arts, of SODEC, and of the Government
of Canada through the Book Publishing Industry Development Program (BPIDP).

Canada Council   Conseil des Arts   Société
for the Arts   du Canada   de développement
                                      des entreprises
                                      culturelles

Québec

Printed and bound in Canada by Groupe Transcontinental. Interior pages
printed on 100 per cent recycled and FSC® certified Enviro School white paper.
Distributed by LitDistCo.

MIX
Paper from
responsible sources
FSC® C011825
FSC
www.fsc.org

DC Books
PO Box 666, Station Saint-Laurent
Montreal, Quebec H4L 4V9
www.dcbooks.ca

for my mother

Contents

Craft

it is nearly dawn as you sneak back in to your house,
where you find them, snoring in front
of the news on the wall-sized screen. you notice he's
in those bermudas, still sitting in a
parody of your past. there are pee-pee-caca jokes about
you on the back of a math textbook,
with your face illuminated by the twinkling afterglow
of aliens raiding your book shelves.
you droid an act of involuble hurt, as you creep through
the thickening light to your room.
the way you hold yourself before the cold bed, comes
with the empty sheets suddenly
sectioned and hovering like so many shirt cardboards.
the red message on the phone is
blinking. "It's me," a stranger whispers, before noticing
a pamphlet on childbirth, done in
a shuttered part of a new clinic. you glance at the bottom
photo, where a single bare-chested
form is dancing on the surgical bed. you realize you don't
know how to explain either canning
or sewing bees in his language, while he whoops exactly

like the sound of your laughter. lifting your knees, you sense
your diaphragm is made heavy
by rounded up change. you feel as if you're in front of your
fireplace that never draws properly.
rubbing your pregnant belly you stare at an ancient fridge,
which is being washed free of
a coat of unfamiliar fungus, before it is plugged in again.
you feel goose bumps as if a

dead hand is brushing across your nape, and you begin to
lose weight visibly and you
get ready to pass out, but you make efforts to focus normally.
a strange sun has reddened out
the details of your kitchen, leaving in a few paintings on the
the walls: a faded blue-striped
awning over the bouillabaisse restaurant where you first met,
a winter sea where you held
between cupped hands a peninsula, where your son was born.
you can't imagine how hard
you are hit by the bend in the rain, where he always averted
his eyes and invariably looked
down from the boat with his black eyes wincing from the large

white medusas, nearly two feet
in circumference, floating and pulsing with the waves. you didn't
believe him when he said they
came to him, dilating and contracting in his dreams like intimate
optic muscles, which taught him
how to build subaquatic spiderwebs as a map to a home reversal.
no close, surviving relatives he
had written all over the kitchen table, where you're lying immobile.

opaline saucers are flying around
you as the door slides open and you quickly curl, rattlingly into
yourself, as your child had done.
he counted on dying quickly, when you tiptoed to your closetful
of others. he bobs behind a full jar

of snacks. you spot two coconut macaroons hurdling through a
set of fingers and a chocolate malt
ball in the other. he's thumbing through the jar making serialized
sugary tails and bug-track vowel
signs, that look like the radiating dots in comic strips that indicate
delighted surprise. you lurch easily
in to a standing position, incuriously offering the cookie in your
hand, that you reckon you just baked.

Decremence

carrying the thin quadrigae half boxer, secerning out its swarovskin logo against the tiger mosquitoes, pitching prickles from the bottle bore floral of the broken blanc de blanc. from the room smaller than the floor below that clears the trees, to the inward curve of the huang he. on the obdurate bites on the back of his knee clusters, he pulls his thigh in to the egestive leg to a lan jai's blood, with the collimate strings plotting routes from the

point of impact. through loud voices crept after the decomposite sketches began to appear below the numbers above the automatic door. as it fluxes at a dimming sideways motion, accepting the peeled back foil of the half-eaten yogurt around portion of his braid, still wet from the resettled toilet batting the quick impressions of the grip of the florence border tee on the middle landing, the lights of night traffic queueing on to its worth saving

in the squaring of his feet in the innerwear, the elevator door opens to the balled-up blanket of jagged plastic from over the coin-use binoculars with the capiche? the door soon bumping up against it slid ponderously, a light palm weighing a softened circumference, worsted by the logged compacts of sacs. in he is to tiumouh to the canful, his face nears to the veiny clutch of the tee on the carpet, with shallow punctures of his hair, cut also shorter

---

quadrigae, a two wheeled chariot drawn by four horses abreast
huang he, the yellow river is known as "the Cradle of Civilization," remarked for its enormous quantities of yellow sediment as it flows through China's central provinces
lan jai, punk in Cantonese, referring to boy prone to fighting
collimate, refers to making (light rays, etc) parallel or adjusting line of sight
sac, refers to "kiss" in Cantonese
tiumouh, colloquial word for dance in Cantonese

Simulation Fledge

nodding with the incensed stare at the hembra in her hand aloft, with the other lowered to the digital roulette miniature fastened to a safianno key ring of bear

as her forehead's speckled lines and roundedness of cheeks appears renitent in a scowl, the eye pillow wedges in the lift of skirt, in the shivering her rear into

the tako plush behind the captain's chair. holding the earrings tinkling when it starts to take off, closing to steady altitude as she breathes trepidly, holding up

her hands to stall the quick bzz-bzz in her ear. with just a blink of eye, sighting the snowflakes added to the stratosphere, with her face pressing in to her elbow

when the breadth of an urn is opened and maundered. as she rearranges herself so that it's out of view, before the record first smile that is verged to a baggage

train porter gazing demurely at the bag, left at the semicircular dive in tsimsha cheui. his wallet's contents are stretched to her, along the filling of the flow of

cargo dress trousers with the sway she's to effect in the glove-ish half-fingered try to tilt loose the bag that is hidden from view in the near-deserted lobby with

the few bills left in the shirt. the high-rounded insteps of blue satin slippers from small feet is felt as she wiggles impishly what seems to be small tent pegs in the

four "pencil" pockets, when in unrecallable sinking to seat, there's screeches of tires. skidding off the runway, as the shards from the cremulator spills, not fully

pulverized. at a jerky stop, she half turns as the inhuman legerity of the adjuncts are obtruded as she puts on her left heel. bent with his bag, promatorial crossette

_____

hembra, denotes the female castanet in latin percussion, paired with the male macho
saffiano, a type of thin leather, cross-hatched and textured, exclusive to Prada
tako, a plush, measuring 10 inches, a plush octopus from Tado's Cannibal Funfair, with
    a stitched-on bandage
cremulator, after the incineration is completed in cremation, the dry bone fragments are
    swept out of the retort and pulverized by a machine called a cremulator, in to a fine ash
TsimSha Cheui, is called the tourist sex ghetto in Hong Kong. While it's supposedly hidden,

I happened to observe a wide range of nightclubs, lounges, short-time hotels, brothels
promatorial, referring to the building in which corpses are frozen at extremely low tem-
   peratures, so that they can be reduced to powder
crossette, a large pumped star in pyrotechnics which splits explosively in to a four pointed
   star or cross shape

Rime

she's casually placed on his shoulders, as the cart holding clean linen is pulled from blocking the suite. by one room and another, vigorous rasping of vacuum cleaners, partly visible gym-slipped forms letting out billows of steam. some inappreciable laughter over checking the pot coaster. something about rhyme as she is a bit piqued by what's worked in the numerals embossed on the credit card, he claps on her

sight of the slotting of both palms vertical, about three inches at her mouth level the tendril of hasma. halting at its drenched appearance he briskly moves between the smoking room and a mirror, while she swivels and he irons out the hold. she notices the carpet soiled along the preterition of the curtains he continues beneath, wheezing against the central stile of the partly opened French door. trying to pitch them

back along the closed part of it. he hurries to the closest lift. huddled in an ascribable laxness, it criss-crosses a huge atrium. by the fanning out of spray water, she's set on the tilted float, pulled by two roundly submerged cetaceans. she feels tottery, unsteadying the outside of his right forearm, to the pertinence of nails in his sleeve, as atlantes with the half-cone on his glistering stare, to a place he doesn't want to say

_____

hasma, a Chinese dessert ingredient, with a granular fatty texture, made from the dried fallopian tubes of frogs

preterition, the act of passing by or over; omission

cetacea, are one of the most distinctive orders of mammals, including dolphins, porpoises and whales, with characteristics including their nearly hairless body, anterior wings modified into broad flippers

Avidity

the water gets shallower, as she entrains the plastic bag filled with the picked of nine-dollar covers and glassines of mares' polls. one reedily neighing on her tread skirting the rocks, while the unbroken kanten is bracketing her neck. flop-eared as she nears the shore, where the low cloud hangs around the weather-beaten corner. her step braced where she was slipped from the stool, in the alacrity of her knee depressions she feels the crumbled deutzia, along the low plastic barriers blocking and turns on the shack's slight bombinating by the tufa being reloaded

sensing shadows come and go through a stretched rectangular reneging of light to her counter's remissness. an unseeable expression to the one she sees out, nicking on the way in the one standing scrabbling with its back to her and she pauses, as creeping past of others jiggling the bobs and bits that fell stream on to some clustering into the wall propitiation it blocks every line to taking in the overlapping grunts, in time with the rhythmical gathering of air, imperative thumped and the tapering like a cut-price air freshener. she runs out with a badly peeled eolus, puckered

---

kanten, is agar agar that can refer to an instant hot fibre drink, tasting like 7-up with no fizzle, like a thick, flat soda in Japan

deutzia, a genus of about 60 species of shrubs, native to eastern and central Asia, including the chardonnay pearls, with their white bead-like buds

tufa, a variety of limestone, formed by the precipitation of carbonate minerals from geothermal hotsprings and other ambient temperature water bodies

eolus, derived from the ruler of the winds in Greek mythology, where Aeolus gave Odysseus a bag of winds to help him on his voyage back home, but unfortunately his crew opened the bag and the winds escaped.

At the Plaza

she narrows the list to two on a rollaway bed, surveying her soft shelled
for a twinkling, as its head thrusts thulian to the substandard nicoise tart

while high tea is continued served in a quadrupedal manner. toupée slid
on the one, prising the sevruga caviar on scrambled egg, she pares on to

a spot to find it's not empty. a mini camileon heel descended two inches
delivered from a section in their porte-cochère, inconsiderable in getting

rain-dampened, while the abounding of bags and iconic orange boxes are
comparably dry. bypassing the pettidress she's to wear, except the hands

together behind the back onesie that is donned, as she waggles her foot in
muliebrous replanning. a phone call entreats the hair bow be readied with

the boxwood comb. the butler by way of ignoring it, is winded by a turtle
not there. into an alikeness of being dragged from store to store, the pace

goes to a claudication to the riding of spivvy glasses up. hearing the door
she looks down to her padded step, as there's the click of an alligator clip

to the radii of unryu paper interswapping with satin ribbon, the strands at
her temple curls damply, till an idling precedently of a korker untrimmed

---

thulian, refers to pink shades, halfway between red and magenta, the term thulian
pink utilized on an array of commercial clothing

camileon, a company who were the first in developing adjustable-height heels,
their shoes with mechanisms that hold feet into different places through stain-
less steel rods

claudication, a medically term referring to impairment in walking, or limping
with pain, cramping

unryu, a type of paper made from 100% mulberry fibre, prepared through half-
beating it to render irregular patterns, as well as adding to the strength. The word
in Japan also suggesting the pattern of paper is like dragons riding on clouds

korker, refers to the curlicue shaped ribbons, that are used by some younger girls
to make bows, at low expense

Dynamic Stability

she holds a cissus plant's burgundy undersides to her throat, scanning the prong setting between the stunted pencils along the spine of the table. her soft pressing on the pad's faiddi hóufàan runs thermochromicly by the compartment container as she gazes down and in, her upper body lurching as back from the bed with the sound of the paperboard top flaps's dragonflies tilted. in her pulling the cha siew glaze on to her rabbet-chestedness, the crossway captions' alarmingly unglanced

even as the vein on his forehead becomes prominent lovat blue, while she covers him, raising the stiff window propped with the waxed cotton dopp emptied of the slip stoppers on the soles of pump socks, hurriedly rebroidered initials, conveyed at the spat-back phylloides. reaching for the box of tissues with an accompanying expression of reaching for his crumpled shirt for his next achalasic guggle. slaver oozes to a muling of his fingers along the glandular tissue left behind. she breaks

to the corridor, where the chapped, reddened hue of her is still up, the unassuming data unfilled. she turns on the light as the mobilicity tone is heard. murmurous by the green plastic baran, utterances of thought you might like the chance and like it isn't meaning that gindóu way. as he struggles to swallow a little, it's the don't do that heard when he wakes with the blanket part just cooled, the tenting of the food in towels unlike patient fare. the load in his chest loosened, the inluctance to let go

———————

faiddi hóufàan, a literal expression in Cantonese of get well soon

cha siew, barbecued boneless meat (usually pork) is a popular Chinese dish

rabbet, a recess or groove cut into the edge of a piece of machineable material, often wood

phylloide, a type of tumor that is typically large and fast growing, that forms from the breast

achalasia, a disorder of the tube that carries food from the mouth to the stomach, which affects the ability of the esophagus to move food toward the stomach, characterized by difficulty swallowing, regurgitation and sometimes chest pain

gindóu, a Cantonese expression meaning meet, see you, as in the expression Ngo hou hoi sam gindou lei–I'm very happy to see you

Costime

falling in with an ani-com group, inplugging their sonys to sockets concealed in valencienne flounces. their tapered pearl-powdered faces amatch with her gentle intransigence with their chirping, wheedling to a pause at a ttokbukgi single line sniffed deeply, the passing of a bag of pungent mugwort down to lie on her palm descried with a misgiving, before it is filling up with a grabbing cluster portably and suddenly so closely moved together that they could not look at each other's chapssal flattening. in trying to make a change of position, a set of red feathered falsies is left quite gummied by the heat of the sun in the hold of shoulder frame

that an argyric raisure of a dop near catches grazing on aster-patterned wrist just as she took her flexed fingers to half-averting the frequent burp-stops. as a hand works the paper out of her purse, another releases the thumbs and forefingers of each hand joined in tight circles, another's soft-reposing the tightly folded piece of prescription with a ponybrass pendant started around the date. she thinks that she doesn't have to say when it is clumsily coronaed, in waiting the store's taller by quite a bit, rushing loose the tied bow in back. while retucking her grey-black waves, she is swirled from sitting in upwards of an easy chair, as in their niminy

likelihood

---

ttokbukgi, popular Korean fried snack food made from sweet rice and various other ingredients
chapssal, glutinous rice paste, often formed in to rice cakes called *chapssal dduk,* which is so sticky, it was dusted in corn starch in the past in Korea
niminy, refers to the expression niminy-piminy, an affectedly delicate, refined, fussily dainty tone

Phone Physio

leastways her prospect a thitherwards a minute before it is broken-off as she listens
soberly to the operator saying his girl not yet ready as there's still part of a bottle of

allanoin lotion unused. requited admonitory stillness she rubs the range with waxed
bread-wrappers releasing an unimprovable series of sighs, that goes a bit squeaky in

hearing a nursery feel of tam tam zhun and that it's too long in the crotch on the doll
and she is to keep on snuffling, as he starts on the delicate twist of the ankles as she

leans to opening the theobroma as the habit of asking the name as she hears, gai zai
is followed at retractile of perfectly flat chest. in mashes of mmm hm to maiasauring

the deflating blow-up irrawaddy's face, creased and helpless and still irreproachably
cute. its bumpy chin staggered on under her brandished mecha puttic statuette heard

counterfactually as the pops made in the spurting slobber out of her sliptoes while it's
heard falling with a clatter. his fingers closed around its throat's moisture his necklets

readied by someone else, as she's encumbered by the suasive end memory capturably
distant, saying she came blundering like wet mai with his rusty-enclosing toy, aghoric

extends a lower lip to blow the tyre-iron from its snatch, yields knelledly lusted stutch
positioned with her bandy-legged gait, interproximal with a vomitus of ligeia's salvo

tam tam zyn, go round and round, the first line of a popular Cantonese nursery rhyme

theobroma, chocolate is made from the seeds of a rainforest tree called theobroma cacao that only grows within 20 degrees of the equator, while there's a theobroma chocolate company creating assorted organic chocolates

gai zai, chick in Cantonese

maiasaur, with its large duck-bill, it is considered a good, nurturing dinosaur. While it stayed close to its young, without obvious defense structures, it's known they moved in large herds as many as 10,000 dinosaurs

irrawaddy, is also known as the snubfin oceanic dolphin, related to the orca that is critically endangered

mai, raw rice

ligeia, "Ligeia," is an early supernatural short story by Edgar Allan Poe, following an unnamed narrator and his bewitching wife Ligeia, In falling ill, she composes "The Conqueror Worm," involving lines of how life is sustainable only thorough willpower, shortly before dying. After her death, the narrator gets wedded to a Lady Rowena who soon falls ill and dies as well. In his distress, he watches Rowena's body rise from the dead and transform itself into Ligeia's likeness

Red Riding Hood

she swears fei hai not to follow her even with her sway, unappeasably varying in close, the disbudded ise-giku abraded with weight attained uniformly. tilting it outthrust against the railing, trudging down to the bottom of the stairs, to a snippy pile of rutilant smocks. reclimbed out of the burnt up heap's stagecape, flailing her hand with the wall's this much for the light switch unfound. she braces on the hum of the squat meat freezer. on top of which the monogrammed butter-pat of a shield is felt nibbed where the chaetura swift was in descent. she abscises the sheerlon to the shifting panoply of wriggly eyes, uncrossing her thighs and in crossing her ankles, the space between her legs half-clusters the chenille stems, some still lain on long sides of felt for the riding hoods

floppily shunting over the involucral bracts, as she skips the flowering still. taking the singly pointing crimson hood at the lot near the ancient gym bag. using the horse-mount steps, a concentrée of bigarade as she flattens on the newer section, bringing her hands down as if to stop the patting. she wraps herself tighter to it, with demonetized, the blows in the whirr of the greeney half-dark. as she's leant forward on the upper cut bag, hearing capital freed of production, exchange or value, profits with the capital managed while the cape secured with miniature forest buttons holds. the disconnected from the real economy with a stepping charily out of onto the rug. as if disturbing the trouser cuffs, the gunge "lai" might escape, as the box of softener sheets falls, she shrinks back

in

---

fei hai, a Cantonese swear word, fat cunt

ise-giku, a flower that looks like a broom or mop; the long threadlike petals completely cover the center disc and hang down

chaetura, refers to distinctive hair-like bristle feathers, projecting from the ends of chaetura swifts

abscise, to cut off or away, remove

sheerlon, a type of latex that is very strong, while made thinner, used to make the Beyond Seven condom

involucral, refers to a series of bracts beneath or around a flower or flower cluster, or a membranous covering or envelope

lai, come in Cantonese

Syzygy

not joining in on the sledge ride, gazing rinsed in his spangly nightcap's plywood escutcheons he removed from the tudor house. at the top of the driveway, maybe stately and more restrained in leaving the heartsease on the garden pavers, then in his extreme youth. a day ago its 10 cm spurred measure, trained between the knee he befitted with knitted cross patterns and where the emission was found. he scrapes what's left, boring into the angered scrapes over the malacia in his knotted knees, unlike the flowing noil on the unfollowably long-lined midge. being scrutinized in a gleeing

when stopped chewing the mini crab roe outlined in the wrinkled chinese character guide paper. snuck from the high-up shelf for winning a day off from the tries at hunan tofu. as she chews again stretching her hands from crystallized headphones to fanning placatingly to a cafardity at the foetor from a portion of his filson rucksack he inspects past the *naihuang* extras while poking past a scrawny gap in the bags. he misses a makeup sponge she takes back. pressed like an asconoidal clod, she raises greater then 25 cm from his flusteredness. she cringes at the grizzle if not from his club-

like ankles. his head cracks back on his neck, a slab of straining forehead to views on the unfamiliar angles of her grin, after it's tossed by the sprig of watercress decoration in remains of croque-monsieur luncheon. as her arms loom just to her sides, disengaging from the left to left again. in his leaving alone, he stuffs the debris of bei si package in to his back pocket. along the rip along its seam, a miniature blackwork curtain is climbed in with his damp cheek, tumbling on to his eye. taking in the slowest breath as they tumble back, a pizzafication of the sponge for a hereafter's house

---

malacia, condition involving the softening or loss of consistency of bodily tissue or organs
noil, a waste piece left over from combing wool or spinning silk that can be reused as
   a decorative additive to other projects
cafard, a feeling of severe depression from French
naihuang, sweet yellow creamy custard filling, applied to some bao (bun)
bei si, plum pellet haw snack (colloquially can mean nasal mucus)

Showroom

picking the sudoku book, where she left off, hearing the grating sound of the sliding into the lock. sipping from the cup's calpis a second time before passing it back by the small pile of pearly eyelashes. organising it in to a decagon, noticing the song needling from the door moderately ajar, with the straps of her overalls slipped to the side while the alencon lace mantilla is spread and she approaches the endlessness of the chants and pitches like an infant trapped in a tool box or the ikemen bank filled partially with coins. to the lcdic form, saying i'll make you happy, baby on the right, the let me caress you crackling from the left as she releases

the holed orbitual weight. then locking to the extra-wide tyrian contacts she tips back with her hand on the cover of the closed journal, featuring cerridwen like the numeral ago, she ran around in ivory makeup kept in a minaudiere, leaving incomplete a hint of her neck's disguisement in a totaling as if someone might be watching with an expression disdainful in the set of the nose's dorsum, lowered brows gouged in phony casket. picking up the roubaix ashen t-shirt, dropping the corners of her mouth to something like her daughter's sweat and something else, narrowed as the compromising of her stole, in the give of wine-soaked wrap of never

opened reproving dress

_____

ikemen, a heart-shaped coin bank from Japan, where saving money relates to connecting to 5 different virtual boys

lcdic, referring to characteristics of lcd (liquid crystal display)

cerridwen, one of the great pre-Christian lunar goddesses from Celtic culture, associated with wielding great wisdom, prophetic foresight and shape-shifting abilities, like assuming the shape of a hawk

Misslay

unsaying her name, while shelving the letter with the luna inverse marque, brushing the stray salt from its ridged border, like the sagnarelli she spares with paneling of their scrawny replums on erysimum pendants. not saying it's been a long time when strewing the coquelicot knee-high tangled with the scrunched belly band from their leon pup. its level bites on the tongue tag, spotted with takumi burger is handled to a cardboard box. cramped in mags' ripped headcounts, inclining to the dun-colored tapwater's pairs of rellenas. out of grooved habit, she garbles the things in a span of standoff

distances. sluing the desk mat cleared of printout of them, with the ample heel spur a betch whatsis, while walking though the turnstiles of the shoe shop, eluding the alarm. to the front of the shop, a plastic tote overturned at the start, the shrink wrap plastic of dry-cleaning, outspread speedily to the block letters nee doh. in groping to the sinuated horse, its poppet feet on the tabletop, instead of curling up the dowels sticking out on each side. again seated on the flat back section of the horse–as she crowds it, saying you should sit here. in donnish bearing it like equals, a sparsity of penates

in bockles

----

sagnarelli, a type of short, flat pasta ribbon, with fluted edges on all sides
erysimum, term referring to wallflowers, including about 180 species
coquelicot, corn poppy, the term applied to the flower because of similarity of color
    to that of a cock's comb
takumi, meaning artisan taste, is produced through MOS food services in Japan, the
    term applied to a burger, made with Tasmanian beef and ten different toppings
rellenas, stuffed potato balls
betch, another vernacular way of saying "bitch"
nee doh, here in Cantonese
poppet, an older spelling of puppet, while some apply the term to mean voodoo dolls
bockles, refers to Ickle Bockles, who produce a series of storage solutions for travel,
    from lip balm tins to the sanistick, an anti-bacterial hand-spray

Put Out

diving in to her berth, listening to her take the stairs down to the second floor, walking inch-by-inch in the shoes of basashi wrapped in butcher string, before tripping up. in slowly backing up to a louvered door on the accrual closet she sees from the corner, she picks one of the seven partially eaten pluot gummies palpated within the bag. extending her muscular forearms across the ledge, she rests her gingival smile near a dreg of grey pleated pant with integrated vagisil 7 oz., looking at the plustache with the hardened 2" x 2" of mobiluncus vesicate. as a shawl is crept short to her lip curling, without negging sick at the billowing cloud of ammonia, in it just not stopped looked at, the ordering an array of wee soft-loopy bags, till the ground bones of lorises uttered, so she doesn't once look up. to the pit of mamoncillo held in a solution of the saltiness and blood from the wrung midcalf merino socks, lifted out of the berluti trainer unprepossessing she unaugurs. letting out a rancorous chuckle, as she fine-sprays her in crumblets of pangaea's horse sausage. this once her eyes moving less under the eyelids, when she views transfixed, a hairless flarper's foretalk in maxillary excess of ban dzou the acidulance 'neath upper lip raised even higher, between a surge, a big braunful

---

basashi, raw, sliced horsemeat in Japan

mobiluncus, anaerobic rod-shaped bacteria, found in the human vagina with bacterial vaginosis

vesicate, to raise blisters or vesicles

mamoncillo, honeyberry otherwise, tasting like a sweet lime with a hint of banana, the pulp gelatinous but scant.

berluti, company that makes bespoke men's shoes, the trainer known to combine the comfort of sneakers in its construction with bootmaking finishes

flarp, refers to a musical toy that makes fart-like noises, flarping becoming part of some urban commons, involving the sound and the execution and the response of the victim

ban, refers to pretend in ordinary senses in China and can be used in the phrase ban dzon won dei, a woman who dresses as a man for a performance

dzou, means to make or making of any number of things and it's included in expressions of sexual intercourse, *dzou oi* (making love)

Guessable

she arrives at the house, pinching the cold trapped in ears
unhinges tansu showcase with retightened gunze sample
carnauba waxen yoke, the pair is checked for striped stains
counted through rilakkuman mask. offering her a seat in
the vestibule, a coarse crackling to the neck of large teapot
unveiled. a piling of whitish i'm sure-hearts. his walk
exudes a crunch to her winding, by a pacing between
bedroom and closet. sprinkling of caseless pillow and
donning of katsura wig. strands snarled with mycelial
add-on, adhering the nits to squint at his demonstrable
epilation of weak pecs. he takes off the manchester shirt
cabling around his waist. he chortles at his mo lei tau
she tries to follow his exposed legs, trembling
under the whirr of shedded nails. quiet trace of her
fingertips to land on his wrist. pixelated slightly as
he links her gesture to remove hip pad. a cyanotic jangle
in her veer in return. a chuckling like disfigured yu fa
picking at clutter of gaffing. half an arm's length
away, a fluoroscope pushed is covered by her fundoshi.
spool heel left slides anechoic, a little glabrous point

tansu, is the Japanese word referring to chest or cupboard, while often used in the West to refer to traditional Japanese handcrafted chests

gunze, top underwear producer in Japan

carnauba, a wax substance used in some candy coatings to enhance their appearance, while also helping to prevent stickiness and moisture loss

rilakkuma, combination of the Japanese pronunciation of relax and the Japanese word for bear, a character produced by the san-x company and true to his name, he enjoys relaxing, lying around, sleeping, soaking in hot springs, etc.

katsura, a Japanese wedding wig also known as Geisha wig

mo lei tau, name given to a type of zany humor in Hong Kong

Yu fa, a friend of Hong kong director Stephen Chow who has done cross-dressing cameos in his films

fundoshi, undergarment for adult males, traditionally worn before World War II in Japan, made from a length of cotton

Tuiping

repeating the walk-and-nod through her bedroom, shuffling the minidresses with lassitude. to a humming faultily to the boynq alibi speaker, at a succus tip of the louixs in the near darkness, left by a pile of hot hair piece in a gait changed from boxy shuffle to propelling a sort of off-duty reflector banding from a running suit. insecurely lopsided aloft the coffin nesting boxes above the clothing rack, where a drawn glinting of a skull capsule is squeezed from the moi-même-moitié blouse. she tumps over some bunched-up wristlets with his stares at the perforated dry lace, sliding an edentated border in to a fold of neck skin, wricked out of the absorption by a slow drub of uroflow he tries to shoo without lifting his hands from the sliver he lifts backwards to a furrowed

cheek, as she licks her index of a seethe of sang choi bao from where the thud at her wrist joint, matches with pickup prehnite mala. while he catches a sight of a hosta bloomer, saying que faites-vous, she pushes the stray hair of the wig over the bioplast stud as she removes it from her upper cheek. it is dampened in a stilting weight of her cheek pulling her lips in to a severe shape, when she recalls following his hand by the half-round bell shade touching the little blobs of makeup. a wet trilaminar triangle of her slumbering bff, in heading the chair up quietly, he squints in to the file of clothes with an arrête, blearily leaning to the crabbed lace stretched. with a kind of muscling in the waist to thigh panels of his trousers. as it goes, but he shields the paronymic resection of his bladder

again

_____

boynq alibi, a speaker and webcam system with its combined design involving the webcam hiding under the top, while the speaker hides on the bottom
louixs, known as the most expensive cigar ever produced by Goldwin tobacco
sang choi bao, a classic Chinese bun with a range of fillings, wrapped in lettuce leaf
prehnite, a gemstone with a distinctive "misty" quality of green, sometimes with black inclusions adding to its distinction
mala, the earliest form of prayer bead, some times called guru beads used as rosary in Hinduism and Buddhism, while also incorporated in to some current jewelry

Nuptial Rites

her hand strokes my hair around my ears. feng-huang feathers hushful with
tied pieces of shuen, tossed over lifelong glasses stuck onto maple branches

i cover the sill with alternating pecan sandies and gummi lighthouse sukha
staring down at fat choy multiplying in the birdbath, as he moves his hands

four fingers used like a fast-moving maneki neko, to her voice insisting it's
time and I'm led. the beaded cerise tassels on corners hiding my looking by

pair of van erp vases, portioning elegance by the dollhouse with its kamado
set she's giving. I peer in to the hearth sunk in the floor, its nearly inaudible

tiny yelp, as his waiting by a standing mirror shifts his black cap negligibly
i lift the kotatsu and blots of heat are tossed against the walls, disarranging

happiness banners over her catatonic refrain in unclosing his used butsudan
with aged buddhic ushnisha smelted to stacks of gold, his moveable rasmi

like a magnifying loupe as he peers through the entrance, to sit on zabuton
adjusting calone impressions in preparedness, while I totter along the room

encircle the dollhouse, as if gathering serviceable indication of its elevator
grille's concentric ovals and the interiority of descent uncluttered from the

corridor I ascend to. I exude the reread of scroll thrown before a takotsubo
as he kneels by the delicate tied cups, emetophobic by the altais, set off to

----

feng-huang, the Chinese phoenix
shuen, long fibred rice paper
sukha, joy
maneki neko, a common Japanese sculpture that depicts a cat beckoning with
  an upright paw
kamado, a traditional Japanese wood or charcoal fired earthen vessel used as a stove
kotatsu, a low, wooden table frame covered by a blanket, upon which a table top

sits–underneath a heat source

butsudan, a shrine found in temples and homes of Buddhist cultures

ushnisha, the three dimensional oval at the top of the top of Buddha figurations

rasmi, ray of light

zabuton, Japanese cushion for sitting

calone, odorant that gives impression of sea-shore

takotsubo, known as broken-heart syndrome or as octopus-jar. It's when you get a coronary attack from an emotionally stressful event, even though your heart is normal

altai, the wild onion grown in Mongolia, deemed beneficial by scientists for coronary and sexual health

Subacution

waking outstretching to foot the waxen jacket, detecting the two-way front zip is readied to go again. in inching and edging the rearrangements of impactions, unhurriedly running her calf over its want of staying sealed. disheveling it by a dropped talita clutch, seen from the rear, coming around as to make it appear it was coming from the direction of its scoop collar in which it'd gone, paused at her short, with the mm ngahm tchees picketing the single-lidded eyes adjusted for negative case. slicking the knitted plops near-shut between her rear, getting jinks in the remove, as she lies glimpsing the coral strip on the bag with spikes caught on house check lining's eupnoea with the bleed of excess wax on to the corduroy collar, a cupran knot hardened in homotopy, with the stride squinting

down a foggy hallway, swiveling the bottle-bottom glasses at the hood resting mediagenically by walls badedly depicting the off-roader and the rented terrier. with her fingertips poised thickly from an abundant distance from her juddered thigh, cubed with the end of night's erraticism. a demurring of pain, with all the sheets and everything coming down on it. weighing an intolerable distance from its adjustable throat tab, making a horn squeezing gesture, dropping only to rise again suddenly, darting finger pollulus with the almost wanting to stop in to tell. inclining backwards with her stayed fingers, giving way to a climbing stiffly out through the airy space. by the set-in bellows pockets, indulgent knuckling at the ungot hoping and not hoping, biosphering the impendencies, undamply flapping

---

mm ngahm tchee, expression said of people in a relationship who are not compatible, who are not meant to be together
eupnoea, refers to normal, unlaboured respiration
homotopy, two objects or functions are said to be homotopic if one can be continuously deformed into the other

Alaya

our ears learn to hear love in the figure, rushing upward over
the moonlit rocky slope, covering the first two. there is no
time to feel frightened. she falls silent, but we can sense
she is somewhere close by, and this bothers us a lot more than
the structure of the one hundredth take. she suddenly looms
up and hurtles past, sending a wave of cold air over us. we can
understand what she has in mind in the metaphorical sense,
but it isn't clear what use all the metaphors are when a ghost
with no interest in us is chasing us, knowing we can't avoid
being touched.

the lines between the cast are not private, they're the same
as the cinematic ground we cross again. he embraces her, the
brush of his fluttering eyelashes crosses her left shoulder as
if to stitch her broken skin. he glimpses at his worried hands,
rotating the dying creature on raised boulders so that she
might present the camera with a better angle. she expects his
palms to hesitate, to waver to her need to steady them. he
repeats his rhythm, lowering his face into hers in a passionate
kiss that battles over her body, as her immortal face turns to
us, impassive.

in the next take, he strokes her cheek, painted the color of
unhealthy off-season raspberries, but her eyes open terribly,
so out of character that he assumes it must be impertinent
showing off. she gets color in her cheeks, coming to life like
a gymnast, balancing upside down on her hands before
landing a sharp descent, pulling up her kimono over him.
he smiles painfully, as she scrambles her plot in reverse order,

so that her death would be the first to go, then the sacrifice, next the romantic conversation, until she ends up with a few nursery rhymes.

the director yells cut as he pulls a wired baby from a slit in her skull. someone brings a fresh forehead on a salver. they repaint her lips a light peach and tipped down at one end, as if they'd been newly torn and skillfully mended. he tries to shut his mind to the fussiness of the taisho-style makeup, creating worlds without sleep. his body shudders with fatigue but dares not rest. a shyness keeps him from telling her, he doesn't want this scene to ever end. she turns her head slightly to one side with a sort of mounting unreachability and he blushes gratefully.

----

alaya, refers to a kind of awareness that nothing within the universe truly possesses its own substance. This concept has spawned many thousands of interpretations. One theory suggests that *alaya* consciousness is half-defiled, half-undefiled, and hence could serve as the bridge to human salvation

taisho, a brief period in Japanese history when a whole-hearted surrender to the emotions enjoyed favour. This earnest passion is now something of an anachronism that may provoke laughter

At Twelve

little to say to eclosion of a luna moth, as she rubbed her eyes with my thumb
she took me by my elbows, while a hug retained along a twelfth determining
question, as I placed the moulton back, saying she can notice it unappealably,
how my serafuku had what's left of neri ami kneaded nether gooseberry notes

i placed sizeably rather near the neck. my uneven desk leg was audible as she
with arms compressed across her breasts, uncurled her milko-chan with slope

of antecollis, along with closed-mouthed smile, as she watched the ever slight
bunching of the flesh behind my arms when I bent to pick up torn yama-uban

flip-out. she took up the pieces of pink mohair she split from a second mouth
at the top of its updo, to chopstick covers left unstirred. each lichun bowl was

pushed back to centre, each I lapped to be colder then the next. leaning on my
elbow, the neck of my shirt opened across a shoulder, her next quiver of half

stares, imperforate. I leaned back on the lambing, as she stretched on ablation
of a roundel on my neck, gingival uneasiness she placed to disclose a pruritus

---

eclosion, denotes the emergence of an adult insect from its pupal case
serafuku, the "sailor" school uniform for female students of middle and high schools
  in Japan
neri ami, traditional Japanese liquid candy with chop sticks
milko-chan, a mammary-shaped plush toy, this one a baby genius
yama-uba, refers usually to an older woman, perceived as hideous in Japanese mythology.
  Her mouth is sometimes said to stretch the entire width of her face
pruritus, an uncomfortable sensation that provokes the desire to scratch

Come Around

she reaches in search of her room. each time it shows itself,
each muffled over-story blocks out more of their saline sun

depth sounder falls from hand, losing contact with ground
the swam air charged with sulphurous inelastic clasping

she places fabric that roughly resembles impulsion 'neath
basement chair upholstery, with its jumbo leotard triplicity

he holds something in one hand covered, uncovering it
from her mouth, an uncooked rabbit milk candy pinched,

pointing from slantwise ink, with accordion folds of a piece
of nylon, pulled outwards. thicknesses of cilia over ankle

the chair jerkily pivots as she shifts side to side, her toes
scrunched, against each incoming sweet's loose sibilance

he tries to closely-mike her inhalation, staring blankly at her
over top half-moon glasses. repointing her toes as the water

fouettes. drupelets of his sweat, moves the abrasion of her
sighs. his ear lobule swelling white as she tumbles from him

to a rock sill. she watches the pale line of his scalp where
his hair is parted. a nemertean follows his bobbing ciseaux

he tries to limp from the stylets, arranged under brackish light,
while she watches in ballon, the water wetting, prying apart

her fears. she advances slowly, his top lip sucked up to his
nose, uncaring it had reached in to his oropharynx for his fatty

emesis. lolling from a cabriole, the flexure of the worm moves
to split in toes. her femoral retroverted starts. feet angling in

to wave processions. she pitches against him, while the waters churn. he assumes actions for the batting ring. from minutes

to minutes, units enter and depart, chased by dermal plasmodia.
coelum smoothed aside, becoming a shivering pas de chat in to

a poorly lit exertion. he holds her cloacal azides, as she can't wake
from his miao asoudocyesis, struggling to rise from benthic soak.

---

nemertea, refers to a phylum of invertebrate animal also known as rib-
bon worms, with their extremely long, unsegmented bodies, some
reaching a length of 30 meters

oropharynx, the area of the throat that is at the back of the mouth, food
passing from the mouth to it

emesis, the scientific term for vomit

plasmodia, a shapeless mass of protoplasm with many nuclei and no
definite size

coelum, body cavity

azide, substance formed by chemical union of two or more elements
or ingredients in definite proportion by weight

asoudocyesis, a medical term denoting false pregnancy, where one experi-
ences the signs of being with child

hei miao, or Black Miao, so-called for their dark-colored clothing. They
were interested in legends of creation, a deluge by drowning.

Already

nearing attainment of her eleven mile bike ride, waning with the snapped back bomber hoodie, as she sets about to dismount, near a variety store, swagbellied with rain. she rode to it, leaving the pursedness of her lips painful, interchanged pucker bloodless. the periorbital circles darkening as she remains apart from the gestured zippered groundsheet suspended toward the window. as the rain slows, she runs the rounded edges of the veil out, from draped under one side, knotting in to a plafond shape. brushing past the labello passion fruit balm and deuk deuk tong, the last drop on a scrunch of titel's paneled nct legging, jeıŋaed. while also a scrunched napkin with a muttabarasaurus. with an episodic memory, she averts her eyes, a mass inserts itself from its salty crystallized scent, called albino nose

pede. moving to continue the ride, another eidetic impression of the disquietude of fast, in the dying days of ramadan. the surge of the body packer pushed to sit upright from her. the bulb ridged door opening, reaching for the tub of glycerine and its little plunger. as inching to the handlebars is paused in the catching of a neck, not quite an opponent's back in dysmetric occursions. again into earaches, the counsel of don't be afraid, as the one called pes tries to drag a leg below and athwart. the word gypset is torn behind the saddle with the line maşallah, as she apprises the tremors in his wrist. annotating the tülü bringing out its front feet to proceed ambagiously to the other. spumous lapping around the field, as he goes to a flap pocket's dime, before tearing to a broad decoration of bat taccan rectus

spills a licensured smile, as he tries to lean it towards her, before turning it away on the abruptnesses of the cazgir, approving its shaggier hump before pausing at its supernumerary digits. almost without looking, he throws out a hand in a shape of conformation, in seizing the pari-mutuel slip, he clutches at the post's hollows. purportedly then down at the perserverance of her trembly fingers over his thenar. a gleeking catenary from a camel's windpipe with each release of its extrasystoles, rotating nowhere, despite its best attempts. rapidly orbital bikewhile, reperfusings where the wujing multiplies nightly at shopping malls, behind sandbags. spasming over his beaded cheek, before letting it sink in to her soaked hair. saying let's lean against the mosque, with thighs slid between the columns, as if already and besides

----

deuk deuk tong, a traditional hard maltose candy–deuk meaning chiseling or breaking
    things into pieces
drunk jenga, a party game involving when somebody passes out drunk, they take turns
    piling stuff on them until they either wake up or the whole pile falls over–variations
    of it involving removal of clothing with the drinking rounds
peş, a piece of cloth where the name of the competing camel is written
Maşallah, means "may God protect him."
cazgir, announces the names of the camels, gives commentary in camel wrestling
wujing, armed policemen in China, stationed in China's northwest Muslim province of
    Xinjiang, where there are tensions

Dim Sum

meet and vanish, my tongue touches inexpertly 'neath a dumpling,
as adrenalin nooses round my stomach. the effect of my blinking
as I chew it slowly is intentionally calm. fondling the flatness of a
napkin and smiling dopily, I add convincing smiles on the front
page photo of Chinese celebrities eating dim sum in view of TV
cameras to show Toronto safe. with sketch-book momentum, I
open my eyes and see the unfocused shine of a metal counter,
while somebody's gloved hand adjusts the bend of a cat's knee.
the waitress dons a mask and her immobilism makes monstrous
her movements. she glances at my empty plate and begins to
slide the empty furniture arrangement toward the cramped and
the uneasy. I lean across the table to stretch out the last pouring
of tea, smiling slyly as she approaches the half-lidded pot. wiping
at the sides of my neck and examining the rusty stains across
my fingernails and she stops dead in her tracks. I try to work up
a fevered standing pool around myself, adjusting my grip on the
back of her chair. "Really, I think I should sit down over here."
she braces herself against herself, as I let out a single cough, before
quieting again. she makes Horlick's in the kitchen in a nicely
pointless way. "What, am I a bad stirrer?" she mutters in a low tone.
her face is lovely in an unfamiliar way and almost grave. I raise
my arms and set my hands at the back of my head as somebody
enters, complaining about unbearable pains in his feet and blaming
it on the Chinese, while another sets down her cat with a shingly
mask. she tries out a coy stagger and we laugh. the couple yells for
tofu buns, that are on the cheap menu, with fast dibs at the last of
the tou-shou sauce. she turns up the gas and places my fingers 'neath
her jaw, so I can understand the kind of time, her blood is keeping.

———————

tou shou, "leading hand" (Mandarin)

Imperdible

A blazing meteorite when it descends to earth is only a stone. The key is to turn the stone into a shooting star on earth. (Sebastian Horsley 1962-2010)

she notices at eleven that night, there's blowing her bangs off her brows by the griddle stage with Ke$han's rehearsal, pivoting slightly as a tyke spins in to another bouncing herself to the close-called space. staring at the black spill of pontefract cakes. as their dropping arcs are chased, she gains on the thrown blob in moving anent, just as they're reached out for in the blackout she feels the bolting of fingers in to her bag, moreover to her combing back educing the twisted top band on the stocking. with the blippeting tik toking chorus, it feels coarsely like the creasing of her nose over the pop-up theatre card. its curtain parting to the shutters closed around 36 skulls, furcately left

on the lone pristine can of labeled waste, cloaked in an ajouré knee. waiting to be forked up by the garbage truck, it's brought up short by the spotlights joined on upright beams. there, occasionally a head cants back to mouthfuls of oronamin. foot wiggling as she's handed a mirror with a gules wear mark where he lodges the pull tab cap, like that found pitched through the aralian pot at her bedroom window. the lights go on to the rattling at the back of his black dyed hair, the slackening of it lavalier as he climbed onto some cinder blocks to muffle the dumpster span. hiking her skirt up to feel the discarded shapes, letting go all that made her blindest up until the moment it happens

her eyes squeezed like in barotrauma, as she shakes her head slowly, looking for the visitors' washroom. maneuvering into the fairly narrow spot with the queue randomly racketing intervals, that bolan lost it at nine, while britney's sun hun whack. as she's leaned on sink, getting the side of her punched hole shift dress wet, witnessless a breach sounds to herself distant. the filings out the uv reactive ink of the Sx's as an other turns herself to the perseids where the underwire rests unclipped, sore and lone-sided. not sure she is the next to go in the stall. as roundedly an impatience, not getting on to this basic thing, for the shift out of her range, the towering black top hat, unnearing what next

oronamin, a carbonated beverage made in Japan with its main ingredient being vitamin C

eye barotrauma, a condition involving small air bubbles getting trapped behind hard contact lenses, causing soreness, decreased visual acuity

sun hun, having a strong urge to do something (Cantonese)

Rock 'n' Roll

I am familiar with this one–blue milkcrate full of suicide notes,
bungee-corded to the back fender, artificially white corkscrew curls
bouncing in his wake like rogue coffin springs. there is always
the clinking of wineglasses mingled to Electric Eye, entranced by
the old electric drip coffee pot with the box of paper filters beside it.
hangnails peeled off, we pile our squealing bodies up against the
door so he can't get out. he pushes and screams until the indiscipline
of a centipede has us all falling. two buttons pop from his jeans and
i find his merkin scaled in my small hand. looking away is the same
as looking, as his mouth in place of laughter swallows it like the way
strange beauty has of turning up seconds before it leaves. he moves
like a liquid sail, his pinkie aloft while drinking an expensive bottle
of water. his song is not done, perhaps never will be done. yet, as if
it is already at the top of the charts, we practice screaming together to
the bathroom mirror. stalagmites of sleeplessness cling to our eyes.
a blonde girl idles her mouth like a seedy-looking cobra around his knees.
another girl produces raised eyebrows, the only social reflex that comes,
as she pulls out another nudie photo stuffed in the belly of a ceramic
Loch Ness monster. the guitar solo scrambles, as I lift his hair out of
his eyes. he responds drowsily, raising and lowering his arms in a
mechanical dance. he freezes and turns, seeming to stand on a rotating
platform, excited that crumbled bay leaves scattered across the
windowsill will deter ants. the broken record loops backward says,
"I asked her for a peppermint-t-t / I asked her to get one." a muscled
lady in a tracksuit enters, lugging a green-tarnished bust of Chekhov
that she picked from a bush, hurriedly tangled in several panties.
it becomes clear there is no music and we're scrunched into a painful
shape on the couch, elephant-deity etched in to our bulk. someone
slaps his rear to egg on his laughing. the blonde lets her hand sketch
out something indecisive to me, between a hug and a double dare.
the music gets louder, the lights begin to flash in turn for a split second,

and I'm held in place against blurring by his swiftly retreating fingers. he struggles over to the low wooden stage piled with the black boxes of loudspeakers. the song starts up again and he hums, "Hey, look, Ma, my chair's broken." he turns to the bed, judged too high to climb up on by means of a three-step wood ladder. sleeping on the couch, we watch his sprouting beard swarm below his Adam's apple, joining the ringlets rising up from his chest, realizing our hit list is in the ghostly atmospheric surf of his breath, meeting our roomy stare.

Electric Eye is a song that appeared in Judas Priest's first platinum album, *Screaming for Vengeance,* that evokes a modern technological environment of high-tech energy and surveillance, perceived by some to be endangering to listeners. The reversed lyrics on Judas Priest's *Stained Class* Album, scoured for Satanic messages, came out with humorous results. The lead singer Rob Halford reversed, "They won't take our love away" with "Hey look, Ma, my chair's broken." The last Satanic discovery in the line, "Stand by for exciter / Salvation is his task," came out backward as "I-I-I as-asked her for a peppermin-t-t / I asked her to get one." These lyrics were unveiled in a court situation, whereby everybody laughed at these subliminal "Satanic" messages.

Bed Head

you stood up, rolled and shouldered the zuber panel with the falaises with the vertical burrows, the subaerial stiflings. your indistinct bend to the padded decals on the twin headboard, impelled in a keeping on its dustless top. a different framed photo in Mongkok. pushed past as the project elevator door was sliding back. your looking straight as if not long enough, saying it was a flub about a gung chong por's pallet

you dropped part-way through the pulling in a léron blanket cover in twists and loops, to expose the siu lai lai banquet invite in the set off box, tamped facedown. as I tried to peel it, you sprang up on the bed in to four tries at gitis catches. tailing off to cardioid heaves in taking hold of the back of my neck. pulling me forward with a towelly hand to an embroidered stub with dew ka ma. what obloquy commissured

---

Mongkok, an area in Hong Kong, packed with shops, highrise residential buildings, restaurants, while officially deemed the most densely populated area in the world.
gung chong por, factory woman (Cantonese)
siu lai lai, refers to Chinese socialites
gitis, a type of Frisbee catch where you move perpendicularly to the thrower and, while the Frisbee is thrown at you, there's a jump. Essentially the disc is hurdled, say leading with your far-side leg, made by leaping and reaching the opposite arm around the outside of that leg, to make the catch underneath, which slams you to the turf
dew ka ma, phrase similar to fuck your mother

Diangerous

she back-tracks one-handedly putting the toast, cut in triangles, with the mused laan fan zyu with the hyaliney white of a shelled pigeon egg skipped on its dot matrixed ellipsis, with the remains of a nail art cane's kiss'll be go from her tender-absenting pinkie. awkwardly, the horenso losing its cone slip, trails down her wrist's garbling to the silver-tone band, yet unadjusted with its resin encased neon nerd pic, carrying the prospecting wasp. as it hovers at her middle kunckle's autogestion, it climbs staunchly as the inlying in nearing an alley emptied of handstyle initials, the faltering city behind busomy dolorologies, unraising more wilfull anonymities. the windows are shut to the rain décapage

as the raw agave coolly tires from her hands, with gerridae leaving the pond's soiled bowl of saang mein. caramelized to her eyes smarting with the last drops, to a breeze seeping speckled, in opposition compounding the breath-scragged lye-water vertices. from her tubing lips' chlorosis, as the muffled rustling of the trucker hat she tip drills the moisture on the molotowed culvert edge, where the fudgy imprints of her breasts were pushed, a pectus excavatum's recedence at the highrise's mechanical penthouse. finishing a coffee in silence, wading crabwise at the sky-level section of what we call "the dot." pushed to a depleted depth of the air seal vertical chase, jamming her knee

in his thigh accidentally as she displays the chancroid like a lahmacun, the oophoritic plangency in hand gesticulation by it, to the whiskers afurled out of his ears in burned hoodylongleg of the jin mao shower attachment. with her unstacked sulima, going to a surety like the fizzy tights, uncrackling during sloping is devised with his inclinometer. dropping the pushed hanger through the center of the styrofoam ball, as her adventitial light sweat changed colour to an ageha's motor lighting system. boles of sleeplessness in unwinced hours, pharisaical queries of her damp hair on his moob tube. imposingly at dawn, the tracings of blue at his clutch freed throat, the azhuic acceleropledge's lock

---

laan fan zyu, a lazy pig (who sleeps all day) in Cantonese
horenso, a traditional Japanese cooked spinach dish
gerridae, an insect family including water bugs
saang mein, a type of thick noodle with a soapy texture
lahmacun, a round, thin piece of dough topped with herbs and minced beef and lamb,

also known as Turkish pizza

oophoritis, inflammation of the ovary or egg sac caused by a bacterial infection, usually the result of a sexually transmitted disease

jin mao tower, literally "golden prosperity building," a skyscraper in Shanghai which is the tallest building in China

sulima, a grain-based alcoholic beverage made by the Mosuo ethnic group living in the Yunnan and Sichuan provinces in China

ageha, refers to a swallowtale butterfly and it's also the name of a large club space in Tokyo. –Recently it's a word used amongst teenage girls in Japan, to denote princess fashion style, snobby mannerisms

azhu, the term women call their lovers in the axia system of free-marriage among the Mosuo

Type

she pauses at the carriage lever, with nystagmic motion pendular over se-dzing, before the viseme of the cracks at the sides of her mouth are hovered with an open and mostly full bag of uka-ru. diarylide yellow crumbs along the ulnar side of her wrist, she insufflates an overstrike

a freshly typed ham pin, she shields as the path of the flavorants fume from her hand, a modulated groan in splitting the front hangs that she slips in to her close-fitted sleeves. he sidles to the sweater hanging on her shoulders shrunk in length, not looking at the slack in platen knob

the space bar sticking, she spills the sheet to the floor where she wipes her fingers. the chip package subsides inwardly as he moves, a lock of blonde hair spreading inches to either side of his lined notebook, near mistaken for a fainted tanhua yi xian. her self-biting for he's, he's not as with swabbing it with the hello kitty 6-color ballpoint, with the cock of her ponytail, held with the fake przwalski bow, on to fragment of the embroidered cell phone case to leaning out to get a calamus of the back-scratcher, as her inquisitive cheek's how much, too alike the long sighs

she expels with regularity. her smile with the dry socket as he mattes the wreath of katana outliner on his fwy rainbow tee, scanning of the rather nervy drumming of her fingers on the armrest, when the nummular rash started, the growing vesiculation and the onycha declined, from a pastel lap and not objecting to the kiss on the purulence on the part in her hair. while going on to practicing the division of lanyards, the tenners supple under his foot, as an erethism twists on the metal hook in erythrodermal diffusings. the strand slides off her labrum's haven't evens in gulab rose

---

se-dzing, shoot off, to come (Cantonese)
uka-ru, a brand of potato chips in Japan, the name meaning to enter, carrying associations with entering university or passing a test
ham pin, salty, dirty movie (Cantonese)
tanhua yi xian, broad-leaved epiphyll, a white flower which usually blooms

at night, it's blossom lasting for a brief period. According to Buddhist legend, the plant blooms only on the birth of divine kings

przwalski, a rare and endangered subspecies of wild horse, originating from Mongolia and China, which has never been successfully domesticated

fwy, FriendsWithYou is a company developed by Samuel Borkson and Arturo Sandoval III on a mission to spread the idea of magic, luck, and friendship through apparel, toys, installations, etc.

onycha, the strongly scented closing flap of certain sea-snails or mollusks that were harvested from the Red Sea for its scent and use in fragrances in ancient times

erethism, abnormal irritability or sensitivity of an organ or a body part to stimulation

erythroderma, a generalized inflammation of the skin, which involves reddening and scaling of most of the skin of a person, sometimes called the "red man syndrome"

gulab rose, refers to an early fragrance / attar, associated with sublime purity

On Her Toes

another two in front of her, lifting her heightened nasal dorsum, above cooling cup of da hong pao tea. gingerly trimmed nails slides against where the infracturing was redone, as he bides the side triggers on his ardillon belt. relaxing the buckle many a time, going on noting with a disdainful pout the steatopygous girl. in an attitude with the grand-ma grab-bar, as if sitting down and can't getting back up, on the stretched out riffling of a boy. he makes several plunges to open his baetid eyes, to meet the bikini reinforcements in places, the cutting off of a taunt in

the looking at the mimix script in her acid violet notebook, not reading what little of diary. beside her arm raised to pass elsewhere a polybiine wasp that moves along the pages of the amour magazine he left rising and lapsing. not obstructing the sliding of a half egg candy with a few nonpareils left in to a pocket. as he surveys the waxed floss of a bikini bottom rolled limply down in a variety of morganatic discernment and the circumspect boy takes the cane with the pommel, uncasing it more. she stands, pushing aside the hounyon flip-flops proffered, on her toes

---

da hong pao, is an important, deemed advantageous oolong tea, associated with a legend of an ailing emperor, cured by it, whereby he sent elaborate red robes to clothe the four bushes from which the tea originated
steatopygous, an excessive development of fat on the buttocks
hounyo, refers to fetish urination practices in Japan–gamen hounyo is "face pissing," and yagai hounyo refers to taking it outdoors.

Awork

a pace in the daybreak to go to her bah bah, walking, scudding a different count by a vestibule's paired pigeons, mugging with the reporting of 6 am from the chaan gwoon's plastic-wrapping blare. a sinuosity dragging tofu skins, apart from the silken tofu in a belly-clutching while fleetly tripping to the foo jook taking shape. round and round where the refrigerated bean milk views on to him warming it enough to draw the resile of a few bobas to flop a fraction up her half sock and she bends before another comes up just over her forehead. one of her hands out, from the rattling of the teeth not meeting, her jacket flap catches the sludgy puffs. except for the collar fastened, the coruscations slipping from limb to limb stops as she reaches

for kitchen cloths sprawled, prodding the batching of tofu custard with its angled gauntness that he stretchers, broadened to the point of liquefaction while she takes up a tofu stick rested by a jar of bovril, balanced on its lid doubled spoons smeared. waited on, she scans over the sacks to the jackie su artwork copied over the tancho, that had tilted a smile to her last month she stickered their puri kuran lines uncoming clean she finds risible on her enamel, while a shambling of brackish juices comes towards him with side by side cups, equably deconcentrated and it occurs in his blunted face that any moment they'll be a count down from three and he weighs it over with eyes half-closed, spastic in he'll do exactly, the reemphasis kept on him as

she passes

bah bah, dad (Cantonese)

chaan gwoon, restaurant

foo jook, dried bean curd

boba, the black beads of tapioca, with the consistency somewhere between jell-o and chewing gum, in bubble teas.

Jackie Su, is a small Thai restaurant in Bremen, which has some Asian street character. There's a smiling like graffitied image of Jackie Su on its fair-faced concrete walls, holding up chopsticks

tancho, a koi fish with a distinctive round red marking only on the head, and if a few red spots appear on the body, it cannot be called tancho. It's white skin can stress badly, appearing bloodshot

puri kura, refers to photo vending kiosks in Japan and the term is also applied to their photo sets, often adorned with colored texts, frames and cute doodles

Close-Up

she places an ant inside a polished crystal, clouding then
cleansing every transparency

it fights by stalling in each of her breaths

in every picture that shows her, she is pointing out of
the frame, insisting that she's waiting where his eyes

flicker between the windscreen and his multiple mirrors.

inheriting his warm, soapy water, with slow jab of knee
and elbow, she collides with so little else. she rises,
hobbling his lengthened hair to her breasts,

his likeness vanishes in the water, as she
inclines the wig to float toward his mention of others

he draws her skipping, at times dragging by the soup
counter, where no-one is left to celebrate his windfall

the fan is turning pitifully slow, as he pulls out the rest
of the big flat balloon, half-inflated with big startled eyes

she isn't quite life-size as he places

her on the abandoned bike
with its motor still running. he hastily dresses her
in his dark jacket, white shirt and silver tie

with a hole for a mouth,
hair preserved with the smell of someone she forgets

he zooms through the red light and times her driving
up the steps, trying

to get away from the cops, leaving the chase, as

one

Ocean Dome

she begins a tulip twist at amethyst edging of queen headalloon,
   placed over his kerion, as he holds his nose to salt-free breeze
regnant with scent of rubber-rings around girths in washes of
artificial sea. the shuunck, unck of the knives in the distance,
while the bottleflies in the cosmetic temple preparation, keeps
his jagged look from flopping. the analyte of its drone with
the aggregate of charolais to limousin with the spread of red
palm oil across her back, where names of foreign friends are
etched, shy of the expanse of scrollwork of pennedness. the free
hand with usable sounds, like aerophagias or other ballonnements
in vaunting her chest such, that gives enough room to tumefy the
   axisymmetric surf. irezuminicly, disappearing in tight twisters,
danced in and out of the pen. as it gets in his eyes, the fizzing
and vanillan rattle, racking the outlined nappy zullens. unlurriedly
speeds as she rolls to catch a balloon extemum of o toyo's garden.
cropping longer still, riparian alongside tensha beads of polyuria
   she places in patches through his tsuke hige. stretch to knocking
him across inflating balloon by choppy fits of san nachi laughter.
   she lies with maillot straps eased away from skin in crushed marble
sand, cropped by the water. the tie-dye cyanophores squeak to
an induration, ruthenium red as his eyes descend along concave
line of the polychloroprene. he can't determine the noiselessness,
when his lips fasten to nadir of briarean leash. he pulls the plasticity
   cavity over his chest tightly, a stubbly breadth in the anti-corrosive
polymer. bungulan amigurumin ramet, where he goes to get phimosed

---

kerion, a scalp condition involving inflammation of the kin, caused by unmanaged
   fungal infections like ringworm
charolais, a beef breed of cattle, tending to be large muscled, producing more
   red meat than fat
limousin, a breed of cattle, recognizable by their golden-red colouring, with an earned

reputation for their manageability as a good work animal, aside from their beef

aerophagia, is air swallowing which goes to the stomach, causing burping, bloating

axisymmetric, referring to an object having cylindrical symmetry

irezumi, refers to the insertion of ink under the skin to leave a permanent mark

zullen, means to ought to, to should, to have to in Dutch. The word noticed repeated a lot in the Zullen Me Waar Weer song / ringtone, with its will we again refrain

O Toyo, a rare court beauty in Japanese legend who becomes possessed by a vampire cat

polyuria, excessive or abnormally large production or passage of urine

san nachi, a Korean dish consisting of live octopus and sauces

tsuke hige, fake beard

amigurumi, knitted stuffed toy

phimosis, refers to the inability to retract the distal foreskin over the glans penis

Subsessility

two men slide in to the velour seats on each side of her, in retaining her basic outline, staring a long while with restrained eyes on the longitudinal series of feet. urged a bit the nimiety of her ruffle hem skirt distorting by the draft and the currents of air effect seconds later by the forcible slamming of the doors. five stops north of the evening's haunchy propedeum of fire ants from the kolinsky nail brush that the malocclusioned cat's jaw kept tipping. the pustule near the cameo tulle flower by her trachea is warily straightened. disseminating below her stomach, separating them from one another, to sensing an aftershave's english clove rose and glancing an upper lip shine. the sweat coating a lot of his perioral area. in a torpidity like slumber, with a whistling liplessly down the line, she pulls on her lower lip, something wandery as another stiff-leggedly lowers a rhapis palm, unsitting himself. in giving it a careful nudge, the knuckle of his forefinger presses against her teeth. briefly rueing in the tightening fit of the clattering car, she takes a seated step out and further while still several stops from finch subway. motionless with the plunging figure of two-in-one carrycot. the multiposition lain back raising one of them, picking the drool like little winces on the unfastened bib. with the bottom second deciduous cap coming in synkinetic smirks comjoined with the croupy adducing phonation. a splintering of the redoubting grins as she readies to get out, with the seized baby leopard teeth from den-en-chofu, for the hand-linked closure of the toe

seam. soon stepping cross main streets, sidewalks emptied sponsion, seeing the scatter of three empty steel reserve beer cans and the chicory toned shirt saying gravy finisher. giving way to a parking lot, appraising the parking-frame of the dodge's passenger side bursting outwards, a starting out with the deep v placket shirt, hairspraying the rips, as the driver's unraveled wait moves to view one of those multi-lensed optical toys in the black bakelite type material. he shrugs, looking for something in the decolored back lit signs. as the shirt is tucked in to his shorts, she sees their puzzled glance to the press of her purse near the many chips of pictures, as the suv proceeds to stop, facing the arterial road. she lingers, aware it's a little too noticeable, the zipper stretched and gaping, while they return to their car, the shirt knotted low on his waist with the femoral viscus passed through a buluselan snag. telling a similar uncertainty from the glancing sagging of open-necked white shirt. in following her eyes, in the dimness, barely making out the three or so tables. the guard's tie finished with a four-in-hand-knot is raised across his forehead's trio of fine lines. the girl with the orange-blonde half-updo stands, starting on arranging her features in to more lilting, upward angles, stepping lightfootedly to each of the tables. raising the bulkily packed purse to the strip of stores, twinkling with safety lights before peering to find extra containers, his index traveling down the pages, while the vajrasanic stillness of first toe of both unshod feet touched erysipelasly, anastomosing ghotal orison

---

den-en-chofu, meaning "garden city" is a district in southern Tokyo, one of the most recognized luxury, residential regions where many executives have their dwellings

bululesa, refers to shops where Japanese men purchase girls' vacuum-packed (but used) panties

erysipelas, a bacterial condition with intensely red skin lesions, with raised borders that occurs on the ace and lower extremities

ghotal, adolescent dormitories set up in areas of central India, where youth are encouraged to experiment with different partners and practices

In Ends

Roland Brener (1942–2006)

on quieter stretch of alley toward my old neighborhood, taking the seldom eighth metres abandoned by versions of women carrying grocery bags, men milling and longan shells sorbent to candy wrappers. bending for the adhering ribbon with the fitted plastic covering, also agglutinant with egg wash on the bao section running a little sloppily. with the influx of persons with those so near the intersection that the pour of guek bo cha is budged, with the withdraw of ip strada case. palladium belt clip's whiff of pyrophoricity, at the dissever of a kirigami heart under strides. quartered like the roseheart radish buccinal hotter toward the skin, from the space tucked, so near the aisle of packaged noodles. with parts of the red kaolinite mask dropped exanimate, and while not knowing the day caesious, the barchan moon's recremence unclutched while hearing through an inhumed potation, yauh go yaht hei, over the scrabble of all-night takeout. the spue to my hands' anhidrosis along lenticular steps to a recess under a dilapidated sliver. ceasing its churn of chloride, kernelate and once coconut, instead of pork fat, the fumes residue ataraxic, while the fiberglass shape sitting there on the other side of the wavy glass, in pants legs flapping around his tibiae is heard pertussive. as if touching the frosted rorulence of first wish-efforts halfway, for the first few moments to practically nobody, but the silicates slow assignations around its mouth. my fingers fanned, appressed for

---

guek bo cha, chrysanthemum tea

yauh go yaht hei, as expression of from that day forth in Cantonese

astaraxic, refers to a drug or other substance that has a tranquilizing effect

kirigami, variation of origami where one is allowed to make small cuts in the paper in Japan

kaolinite, a clay material, often used in face masks due to its natural electromagnetic capacities to clear excess sebum, dirt and impurities from the skin

anhidrosis, the inability to sweat in response to heat

Virga

she loosens the hanae barbie's stole and gown
looking closely at the consistency of its arm glide
trying to turn it to wipe the rejected wine on her
piquant smile. maderizes as a set of scarlet nails go
aloft en couronne. taffeta spiracles not staying in
place, as her breath makes its way with mastalgia
amidst shambles of re-sifted hangars. serriedly
flicking what she is to wear, burying her smaller
areolas' pleats that peeps through the undyed
faroese boatneck, triply plied over the periodic
achalasia, moving a hand evincing rise and subjacent
screeches to collect the diet drink as if topped up
with tizer ice. she is reached to intercept the pavé
heart top, friable the like of which cannot be costlier.
with her stenotic pose freezed, in disensnaring
the alerting croak congruence (pop, pop) with
raiment carvery. eased again to linedness of (kraaaak,
ah, kraaak, wuhngwo) to an indisposive adjustment

holding panniers uncushioned, brusquely pinching
a corner as she butts the small bites of button kebab
where the boran is to charge at her with blood-boltered
treat dispenser. its denta ridges spread with windsor
red, the complexion of the show while being stood at
a haggard crouch of the garnet sheer front and back
yoke of dress, in which she is to stammer behind the
other, turning right when the other turns careening,
leaning left when the lurching other leans, so that
the frontal one's zombiery would not see the inumbrated
falters of knife pleated bodices, the maxillary trains'

debulked journey. unaided at the procession's head
when a lirral stagger with bristles efferent from chin
is projected with the ballgown flared open to ballsache.
  inches below the turn-ups of her bathetic gown, avers
the fast volunteer's nomingia. in the ubeity of hard-up
blood, as the pygostyle girdle is transferred over her side,
distempered poise sorr-porching heavy richness of slavers

——— ———

hanae, refers to Hanaie Mori who's design was rendered to
  clad a barbie in her name. The doll is clad in a black lace
  dress, embellished with golden woven accents and pink taf-
  feta butterflies
achalasia, a rare disorder of the swallowing tube that carries
  from the mouth to the stomach, causing backflow or a heavy
  sensation in the chest and occasionally pain that mimics
  heat pain
wuhngwo, refers to change or move to in Cantonese
nomingia, a type of dinosaur hailing from Mongolia, distinc-
  tive with its pygostyle-like mass of fused vertebrae at the tail
  end, arrayed as a feather fan. Such a structure has only been
  found similarly in some birds
sorr, silly (Cantonese)

By Puroland

a friend makes a teru teru bōzu from what's left of the polo-shirt
   found on the tile floor, using its flat ruffle along the v-opening
   for a syrinx. curling against the window, noticing as he turns
   another inside out, to position the hoop with no back, the sides
of sleeves underneath. another ignoring the red at the crossroads,
   while inching forward anyway, leaned close to the pitched-back
headlock. on the slant beginning farther right, crossing over the
   sellertainment form's hypertelorized eyes, the myokomia of
where he contorts the occlusal lack of mouth with the exanthem
   of holey red ribbon. undermining where the box sat, containing
   the latter half of the yung yi lei. afterthought as she doesn't turn
   when he trots back down the stairs. as he idly moves away from
   it, the upupan feathercut quaquaversal to the thousandth time,
back to the grid, the waiting freckled fisting, the plumbeous ruts

before the rondure of the limbs in an allocating slide with shards
   of silica, as she pushes the tanuki plush to find the grozer. he
returns, getting to a basket skewed with water hemlock leaves,
   pulling the fasciated applique three rotated 90° under the hook.
   as she reaches to the band where the left ear on the same head
   drops farther sideways. another vehicle backing in, with kittied
led tail lambence kept on. in leopard-print pin-heels, she staggers
to the eburnean ovaloid. the blepharitis of her eyes pressed narrower
then the kitty's temerarious own. dropping the puroland bridal bag,
taking out the white sharpie, to mark-in calvarial strands. qualities
   of static as she nears the enhyalophaged bow. recontinuing as she
   weighs the declivity. glass poking through like on the batiste of her
pinch. for a gokkun balloon she says, jesting anecdotal and anisotropic,
   leaving sokuteic ciliary bands on it, with latest duane reade bandages

teru teru bōzu, a little traditional hand-made doll made of white paper or cloth, hung outside of the window by a string. This amulet is supposed to have magical powers to bring good weather and to stop or prevent a rainy day

myokomia, an involuntary, spontaneous and localized quivering of fine muscle bundles, within a muscle, causing *twitches,* cramps, sweating

yung yi lei, literally means to easily come in Cantonese

upupa, a colourful bird found across Afro-Eurasia, notable for its distinctive array of long feathers, like a mobile crown

hyalophagia, consumption of glass materials

In Ponpoko, the player controls a tanuki, a Japanese racoon dog, reputed in Japanese folklore to be mischievous, shapeshifting.

sokutei, (literally, "the process of measurement"). It's common for stars' bust- waist- and hip- measurements to be broadcast to their fans. But Japanese sokutei typically takes this much farther and much more rigorously: nipples, labia, and more are measured in some cases

Day-For-Night

she carries in her hand a box, and in the box an approving nod, and from
the nod comes
a lonely shrug. she lets off a balloon to a girl who becomes noticeable with
the help of wires
attached to one end to the crane, as she makes a full circle back with it
before advancing up a tree.

flopping her body up on to nowhere until it is comfortable. she makes up
secrets to
tell her and she makes happy silent faces while they wait for the recorded
voice
of a fight to come again. she lets go of her hand and they fall apart.
closely
clustered house fronts and the black pavement appear illuminated in an
unnatural way.

she sits on the spavined basket chair.

a large jianghu stillness in her eyes till she thinks she recognizes the length
and cut of her hair.
teps round expecting to find her reach in to her robe for a golden projectile.
in the distance,
a person's shadow jumps from locust tree to tree. motionless, the dagger
stowed
near her bosom floats towards her eyes.

she closes her eyes, feeling a slice against her cheeks that didn't hurt. opening
her eyes,
her feet feel numb, shrouded in mists, the dagger lodges in the corners of
the walls,
in folds of pillows, metastasizes from plum flower to over-watered lotus.
staring it down, she wheels around, too late to catch it ripping the
promotional figure,

practicing palms. unexplainably, she draws closer to her,

unstops an inflatable gourd and takes a large swig from it. they dodge
in variations
of leaping upward and stooping down to hover above a ring of chairs,
arranged
around a vegetal bed. they hurriedly raise their arms to block the blows,
but it lurches
in to a medicated suction at their index fingers, streaked with cuts from
garden shears.
she brings her fingers down to the most adhesive branch. the other strides
to press
the mattress.

the tenth revolution of a crouching form in the springs,

a bend in a right arm, making a circle with a right palm. the other's palm
strokes
go shallow, like so many sticking plasters, detecting the blanket leaking an
unfamiliar heat.
they push through the covers, fists clenching. drops of rain materialize

sheets unproveably used. they stand side by side. one springs to the right,
the other to the left,
scaling a series of insubstantial dwellings. qing gong along the hangers,
they ease

back into their clothes, fanzi behind their tease.

---

jianghu, the world of outcasts, term used in ancient China
qing gong, ethereal flight
fanzi, secret agents

Thrall

sliding open the door that gives on to the solarium, he coils the string around the drum, shuffling a new tinplate pygmy jerboa. stopping by imprint left by her boot, sclerophyllous branching. inking a euphorbia by it with "all in nei" eight hours passed the whispered fatt ngap fung by the light emitting propeller outside, the stilling of the contusion of her eye, black sclera on background of pale green begins to decussate, while some recall the crisper skirts of the potstickers. the squiggles of reduced cream and the bracing rush of wasabi oil left where they steal across on the balls of their feet. sequencing to dispraising-mime coded hand signals with the ones on the right, with the tweedly pornographic leads over one another. with the projection of the neon lights anonyme of topless bars. the skeptical speediness of demands of a new leng doh boa keng, as the high tensile cable in phosphorescence brings a gharial slider to rasp against the physics of the atelier's door fought. its croaks and throbs, the lancinate male giggles, patched together to hearing his knees drop, recalling the event's arrival of old friends on-linenessness, she has always never been there. going in the direction of the opening door to step recurrently with the capsule, as it goes to where unciform coutil covers a ratite, with a couple of bungled rectrices she has made. the effort to log the pelletal scents of her quim on pedopennal pinions. reshakably the duplicature of a wingstrike with a pawning-alike vagile, outlined in marker on the board balance trainer. dropping it, scraping at the serosanguinity on the burro's mashier bottom, nightscribed with only disobligements, cooing an also-ran to the next scutal aestivation

---

nei, you (Cantonese)
fatt ngap fung, to prattle aimlessly; to talk nonsense in Cantonese
leng doh bao keng, so pretty the mirror shatters, in Cantonese

One Evening

from the mezzanine, a rhythmic additivity in the reflection of a pinna with an earbud being listlessly removed. she hears not the savoring of aji, scored crosswise. mouthing it in less than quarter-minutely rolled love-pes bottle of j'te le laisses. exploring her lips with a slow tongue, barely noticing the trifocal arrayed inside out drops and dabbed on its bulgy lens as a culet. in cheilosil scaling, forbearing to apply the rose trail of the terry baume, in viewing the petrolatum from the red clover and cow's head on the lid, to the diastema's clogged hericium tendrils remaining from yesterday's got of a good distance away. she mimics a fatigue in her torso droop, taking the sticky-out bits of skin mutedly to the underflesh of her crossed right leg. he stares at a silver breitling, before askip to her overlayer of voile, with bands of pintucking on the pannier. behind triclinic slabs of moldavite, declaring can't have that, to the infinitesimal suppression of intestinal pocket, aerosolizing like something he crumples at the bottom of his pants pocket. reaching at the small synres of perineal strands dyed lilac, that he allays on to the upraised bend of arms, slapfull of unnecessary air, as he asserts she's nothing, mong me ah? as he goes on she ain't profitable. she subheads what lilt to tack to her motion when the spoon with a sodium alginated pearl nears her hamate. dissolving like polyvinyl alcohol to rubbing it, watching a slip of balance, in a sort of gerdungernut move. unseating in likeness of durophagic climb, knocking carrot caviar on his lap. the fast variation of cursealikes of brownswards drizzle. as if bulging into the whisked fret, his head broadly down to shush the other perse buis

---

aji, a Japanese jack mackerel fish, which can be eaten as sashimi or grilled and
    served at breakfast
mong me ah? the phrase what're you looking at? (Cantonese)
bui, cup

Inappropriation

a re-orientable step forward, left alone on premises with a wooden sofa, under crowded, with the lap pillow. the creases in the hem of the scabal skirt is crumpled in patches, as there's a suan cai rosette dropped on the polyurethane calves. underhandedly set beneath its folded thighs, while beating time, with the end of her middle finger at a scission in the foam, bungled along the bicondylar joints from the kaho watanabe broadcast. the exudation of the devised septate from under its skirt, as she unpeels the si-chan's overlong pads from the newsprint, to a tortilic print of her palm, plastifed to a submental crease, as she leans over it to arrange the excess of clamming torchon of tête fromagée, with the strips of skinned tongue aggregated near its atresic left. the aduncity of her legs recalling the salophiled protrusion of its mons seeming syringomic. tireder taking the bits of mochigome gluier in spittle to the invisibly reinforced baker's cyst, as she can discern the tenga rolling head cup, leftover. as she feels the flexible rolling motions at the top and murgeoning with the pistonal motility at its base, the pressure such to the markedness of the mimmied

push style onigiri shaper. the network of its blue ribbon on its right ear, while her hello kitty things always red ribboned on the right. she twists the tendony head gland, along branching onto one of the legs, flattening a finger on its passive seated tuberosity, that's minutely porous. fidgety palpitation of its halting no longer fitted with her thoracic breath. yet the synthetic cephaly so finely seamed where it comes apart. while pressing it on the sides, wanting to put it down, on spotting sororal-rectoed mini-t, afore spreading its cheeks out, crankling over to the meatuses' insipidity

suan cai, a traditional Chinese pickled cabbage, that's compressed

Kaho Watanabe won a beauty contest in Japan, as having the world's sexiest butt

si-chan, refers to a real doll from Japan

syringoma, benign skin-coloured elevation of the skin that can be found on the cheek, armpits or vulva mimmy, Hello Kitty's twin sister, who wears a ribbon on her right ear

tenga, the rolling head cup is intended to be used with the woman positioned on top. Fitting on the penile head, its flexible mid-section allows the 2 halves of the cup to move independently

onigiri, a common food in Japan that literally means taking hold of (something) in your hands. These rice balls are made with shaper devices that press on freshly boiled rice, so that it's soft inside and harder outside

Vagustuff

she reaches for the dress in silk dupion, with the contrast ribbon incurved
as it is pulled with her in another direction, to a frequented back stairwell

by the haul of knightly tunic and wheely caltrop. she scans the openwork
of trunks and the ground floor of the sanctuary, with the zig-zag away of

her bicone back dangle. a barbell spacer is moved along the teensy nave
and it's out of focus, in the roll of her head around with closed eyes right

as the blare of the procession starts. a dishcloth with its elastic is thrown
halting them on the meridian of embedded copper. as she wrestles past a

grey hooded duffel coat and the braying ringtone, half listening as they
go through it again, she twists the hairvine avulsion that it is always the

same magnanimity. not saying anything in the facing front, swinging of
arms, a song to which she is to move her lips only in the spangly wings

look the liveliest fixing within a few strides to the doll and she stiffens
in front of the camera one of them has produced, confident it is not the

one that is supposed to be there. suspending the cloud in the organised
way of angel fraise, aware noone will come at her in the same manner

interruption, feeling the friendly cuff on her arm, the cauliflorescence
of one of the faux furred sheep. as the appearance of glass eyes close

in the specular properties of arms outstretched, like the sputterings of
the last night she'd thought it'd be there. her shuffling with snowblind

pareidolia from the passenger-side footspace. the closest she comes to
stopping by the xcite cellphone store, where the egg trembles slightly

and briefly candling its notochordal curvation. with a dystocic chuckle
as it appears fully-feathered, walking and tumbley on its hocks. as it's

handed to her, she holds it gazing to the emmetropia in its eyes. as he
turns to take the box from her, she stares at the orpimence, while it is

being supported to fill its crops, with the gurgling as it slackens, flops
the parrotlet's simultaneity with a jejunal distension pain. dismotility

as her mumbled go dzek with the swingout feeder, the tentacled bird
toy shivering back like a sea pen's. a popsicle-ladder-utozooid breaked

as she's halfway in to one of the circuits of the manger, she splays the
nainsook collecting in the partage of both hands, just until it's all gone

_____

pareidolia, a type of psychological misperception or illusion involving a vague
  stimulus, being perceived as
emmetropia, the ideal state of the eye in which no refractive error is present,
  something clear
orpiment, having a lemon-yellow colour and a resinous luster, used as a pigment
go dzek, that

Another Night

tossing clouding, turning colourlessness, she smoothes the passementerie ends of the train, trailing appetent chondrules between hemstitched space in the case. eiderdown layers on the count of lying tethered intently, with the fea beaalike-plush. the iwako eraser end of a long pencil used to push the fiberfill into the leg is felt a lesser extent firm. the tiny bendy polymer of closed hand, to the quonking of the autocade's sounding of horns with the large pink pearl found in the wallet handed to her. opening the d-eight the beveled end pokes from its gusseted pocket. the residue is found fore-scattered from a hand on her illotibial swell, quaggy from the seated dead lifts of the bag, faintly embroidered with a hibiscus logo. as if weighted in

the repetitive bend, eluding its self-fall, going dipyramidal in the gleam of a mass of tsuruga castle taxi illuminations. her hypoglossal patting against the blebbing of white seam binding, cut to a tooth shape. she is reversed to the right a britchy pastern sliding by her everted leg, as she tries to feel the epulis, pedunculated slightly her short lingual frenulum to the serosal tone of the red ohian blossoms, layeredness over her flailing, made up for too in the wreathed plumeria sap. at a break in the yamamban morning, the clasps of her fingers on the linens in moving close to umbonate again. to a furling farther further. she occludes the tiny amount of light between their rostralic doze on the sheet's aseptic white, a warmth along hyposmic grate of pikake

waking, unnoticing

fea bea, is part of the uglydoll line by creators David Horvath and Sun-Min Kim. The classic handmade doll is 14" tall in polar fleece and 100% polyest

iwako, a line of erasers made in Japan that are environmentally safe, coming in an array of colors and shapes, many resembling food, while some as animals and vehicles, some like a puzzle

yamamba, means mountain witch. it was a youth style form in Japan with it's early manifestations influenced heavily by Hawaiian patterns, with leis placed on necks, ankles, wrists and hair. Their style tendencies involved stick-on earrings, bleached white or synthetic hair, doll accessories, thick darkened and colourful florescent-hinted makeup

pikake, from the jasmine family native to Asia, their tiny white ball flowers often used in Hawaiian leis

Desolation

you say there's a collapsing of all the weight on to you, so that you're
nearly leaning off the bed, running your fingers on the chateau petrus
left against the carved fu-dog leg. not looking back with a choke sung
smile. you urge the bottle to where the foraminal area would be if it's
directly over you, moving it sternotomic till the briskets are addorsed
in the temper-loss with the ironing board's steam system, sending the
heat too in to the sudarim with the balut broth that ducked him to a fit
of sneezing. splatty on pinkney's wretched duckling's inwardness of
too ugly even for a dog to eat. his ha chi traveling, quacked cateredly
to the shook of her shoulder in the dotted swiss of the bed jacket. the
sniffled laugh, when he picks at the supposed stab of a bill lodged in
the tucks, pressed in opposed directions on your bodice-curl hovering
at the cygnet's chased and pecked, told the neck feathers can go a bit
red if it's in areas of iron rich food. while leaving the pond, before it
gets to refuge in the cottage with the cat and hen, it's catching a view
of the water with your flattened swirl of hair hemostatic at the twitch,
as he runs his fingers over the voile of his thighs and she traces where
it's pulled in the humps and valleys at your thoracic cage, as if fearing
the crunch of tiny bones splatted, more the small ripple of egg, like a
thick soup he flits, rearranged to the belonging season and its feathers

lanced. the exalted glide towards, antic with its eyes buried like your
own, overgrown and disordered coque to the cobs' bottomless chests
their nick-ricking snaps and rutilance of spit on unfeathered impacts.
for a moment in a roll-over, with a new-found budging of the covers
pulled over slowly in laps, exaggeratedly pressing valvular raises to
the lapsing back in to position. with each epigastric constriction, the

soundless distance remains as you take the 6 litres to apply pressure
where a rescuer would usually go, eructing the we are too tired busk
while tilting up, with the still not moving, finding your arm to wrap
around it. a more determined repetition of this somnolent gesture by
the bactine aping his navel curd, before burying your head between
your arms, stopped at the continuous unanswering the regal retinue.
as they became stockier, squarer with each garment unloaded to the
slip shift's hem, gathering like the rolling of the cylinder of guinean
feather cloud. the dark base of your mouth's xerostomia as their lips
were pinched with choreic smile summonses. with the black-sailed
pother's droplets, they stood in the amazement of her silence, while
the infrared pomanders of their lips' dummy runs at the yashmak of
brume. as the trailing edge of the sheet is pulled from the squeamed
frenular delta tissue, loosely left. the juk neih hou waan vacuvinage

---

choke sung, an animal, sometimes used in swearing expressions in
   Cantonese, with lay but si yun meaning you're not human
sudarim, sweat cloth
balut, a boiled, fertilized duck egg, consumed with the nearly developed
   embryo, popular in parts of asia
ha chi, sneeze (Cantonese)
juk neih hou waan, expression of have fun in Cantonese
Vacuvin, is a sensually curved carafe that chills without ice

Make Do

take the almond milk she says, in the preoccupied rounding voice of
someone reading the laid down paragraph from the end. shoving it in
the drawer closed with her knee, twitching by the hooked rug's snap
of varied heights of loops on the wall. opening the one above it, with
the slight silkily salted scent of ankimo brushed from the unsteadfast
pattern. back when its blood vessels were taken away, an anastomisis
as she removes the stick portions of the enamel hair fork, sticking up
of the handleless cup. filmily soured, the ornamental tops' cascading
beads, like the heavily keeled tail and the motion of coastal grooves
ineluctable enfeeblement, besides the prickliness of pine and spruce

needles, with the same flat of the blade used in curling the liver in to
a tube in plastic wrap. feeling the soggy, coagulating package. like a
a sort of nigarimageddon, bumptious against the advances of rotring
ink on the stacked stationary. surveying the nib assembly split while
the threads of the ink reservoir no longer sealed from a vernal gloam
its tail flopping against the hold of lobes, sliding the knee to the side
of the grindal worms. letting fall the nijiyan cellophane on the thirty-
some deposit in the night. under barely fictile leaf litter, making oio
eyes at the toes proportionately sooner burrowed, with the swing of
percebes snag. gimcrackery of chutoro at her conscientious hang up

wei. turning to the backyard's upland pool, that noone actually went
near, catching her hand from a dyspraxia, nearly dropping the wood
frog eggs' lack of an outer matrix. a greater quietness, in opening the
casement window, there's less piping whistles from the peepers or in
wood frogs' quacks. overlapping her billowy neckline as she checks
the unanswered rings, the agitation of her jhumki bangles jingling on
the feigned listening, as to the just told her about old al packer upset,
so differs from keeping the salamander from elapsure. anosmial jolts
and néih sédài a? cupping the bog temps again, amidst returned bridle
backed letters and the piling of degorged plates, gustling but to depart

ankimo, monk fish liver, likened to foie gras in Japan

nigari, a concentrated solution of various salts derived from the word "bitter" used on tofu

mageddon, a comic book character that is a war machine, created to make sentient life forms destroy each other

nijiya, popular Japanese supermarket in San Francisco

oio, bug eyed vinyl toy by Doudoupop

percebes, a shellfish with a long, leathery body, appearing like the neck of a goose, with a texture of small bumps

chutoro, belly area of the tuna, moderately fat

wei, hi on phone in Cantonese

jhumki, means "hanging earrings" in Hindi

néih sédài a? will you write down? (Cantonese)

Namely

the girls enter the storefront on dundas in single file, parapraxic in settling to
 the laptop's small picture, the size of their thumbs, on windows in their turns
of polycarbonate.

kind of bubbly through the raindrops on a porch screen, as she notices the crack
started at the dock connector.

out of a power slider case, concealing the small extra sticker from a purikura
 sheet, under a table topped with rustled flat bottomed chip bag.

barely unsealed, the buttered onion spoor in their breaths on overly chewed rusks,
 that it could be by silkworm pupas in the stewed, offaly expression they raced
up to on his lined face.

in their grabs to finishing the food, before the she has already put it on, the first
 holiday day in hongdae.

the pvc uplift top's harnessed sloping, un-evened still, with like a scopophobic
 lurch as one quickened to the hipstamatic close to her.

snitching over the smears that he should be wanted by interpol like assange. to a
 kind of gluier salep, their loose footing over the lipstick bow straying on the philtrum,

the other tips to a lengthwise bite off of the waxes, cleaving to his piqué collar.

the elder of them rising from the wooden chair, seeing the expanded cluster of
 nuomi rice in the six, approximately the figure of the underarm shield that was
sent ahead, nuzzling the dwarf anubias.

the other broods in a slower aisles' sink as she flicks some nepenthe with the
 um sai pa scrawled plum across the mucid "i" in the back housing.

the mod, encased in black tian is swifted up, taken from the wrapped hundred she supposedly got, from the slept in old man's shirt, bean tai mui, like how scratched the front bezel got with just pocket use?

not looking back in their scuffling at the last choucroute ostensions of the bag.

in their basel tears, snagged on the hid phone ridge where the plastic had split,
  re-forming the circling in the seeking section of the classifieds.

an asteatotic caption's bination samely aughts

_____

purikura, a photo / sticker booth that contains an automated, usually coin-operated
  camera, decoration and print functions
hongdae, an entertainment area and clubbing district in northwest Seoul
nuomi, sticky rice in Cantonese
um sai pa, don't be afraid expression in Cantonese
bean tai mui, a perverted sex girl (Cantonese)
asteatotic, a type of skin condition involving dry, cracked and polygonally fissured skin

Summitting

the tip of the caster cigarette from her chelitic commissure, easing over the bottom case's darcel cyclops's character. the simple small roller and flint's laminar flame's regularity hanging down the thryoglossal mangetout sides, where before there wasn't pain. to a parping of her trunk's waistband while careening to the grippy microfibre at ankles. distended with double started knot's aglets loosened. fraying slightly more with the heat cut tags, pinned along her kermode bear hand towel with belt loop, with the red raw pads of its paws snicked slapdashedly. while arraying the motormother t-shirt bursa in the interlocked cotton of camarena silver. like drunkorexic with the recent home from police station's celebes macaque mold face mask, she hikes over stapes popping, where she had placed a shooter's ear protector, a light circlet left from the middle of the doughnut. unlike the toasted okara, crumbling by the set of pickup sticks and the adhered "keep calm and carry on," which was untaken. the slight arrhythmia to the burn in the vocalic tremor in passing her

staring to the black ugg catch-ons, still drenched from the detention behind the cops, while dorayaki is added to a lunch, the tissue off one end of a silver wand sticking out of the ash tray is tugged stealthily, with the karabiner of a pitysing picture. glancing at her pulling the rain-imbrued page from a pamflet zine from the gentle ribbing of the feminy editorial lines on inspiring of new makeouts, as the hiding of the dryades consumimur igni in background arms arcs of peaceful effort, with the rear-splitted skirt's bisecting the longhandled brush, by a sort of shimmeringly stomped makkoli bottle. reaching for the nearer edge of humeral hump of sob, strangled, watching her take the bright okotani earmuffs from her schoolbag, overfilling with bridget everett-like wear. at fake snake-skin bustier, regrappling like neckless podgy, prantic head laid cross the accoach of the same walks on dreading knees. by the arching of the disarmal cushions, support sling unasking if her nei mou had a good time in last night's corner column tepaltion

okara, soy pulp, substance from insoluble parts of the soybean that can be used in recipes like donuts

dorayaki, a confection made of two small castella pancake-like patties with sweet bean fillings

makkoli, sweet, tangy, snow-white Korean rice wine

nei mou, beautiful mother in Cantonese

The Sorry For

she fills her pink plastic cup in the bathroom, walking to the heap of half-dirty clothes. she sits on the shallower side with proportionality of middy blouses with side zippers to curb impact on the slush of the lymphedema. listening to the rain, she uses the bottom of a sweater to brush the eyecup of tong shui on the small ad in the back pages of now weekly, leaving the face flushed with perspiration before leaning to pulse 24. records a t-back where the rest of the rhinestones sewn to its sleeves don't hold, where the phosphor dot quality of them seem to blur over the said last seen near kim moon bakery as if she had just come from a no-show, starved for gye mae bao. as it goes back to the anchor's incipient buoyance at the samban gain in soccer to the left off pattering of rain as she rests the purse she straps to

the center of her stomach. unbuckling it with a hand on its base, a pitch as it is steadied by her hip, but bearing down as the alacrity of the aerosoarer falls in final circling, arms outflung, chest up while she strides the several same blocks, stopping by the dumped gravelly berm climbing up on it just as headlights come up behind her. turning her face to the street and smiling brandishing the right wing rearing-up with slats as the tinted window hums down. she leans in to the pagani zonda, at the driver in front of the glass as the backdoor is pushed open from inside. "rich zai, huh" she says when he edges along the leather seat, moving awkwardly. the car abruptly veers too fast as he tumbles across the seat in to her, as the reflexion of her tired eyes in the sheepsfoot blade coming toward her disappears. she bump-jumps on

to her top's back, beside the touchdown of plastic rigidity, panels flying off, her thighs aching as the car slows. she turns on her left side, in her attempts to propel herself up, holding the updraught, the violently levelled wing in it seeing the lights of the car forwarding. she pushes herself in to a handful of earth and getting up. hearing it's coming down too fast for safety, rushing in each direction seems comparably contorted, as she grabs what seems easiest chucking the set of silver keys as if the nose of the car is nearing her while it backs up until waiting on the street. she feels the decreased heft of her purse, squatting down to get the one key in the prism of the sprinkler spray, a silent arrhythmia making out the shear line, unanswerably pressed to the nappes at her heart, in noticing the waving motion of a hand to indicate that it's all fine

_____

tong shui, refers to a variety of sweet warm soup, custard
gye mae bao, coconut bun
zai, boy

The Call

he hears the receiver drop and her yelling something wildly in to the background. it bumps against the counter, once, twice, dangling on the end of its line, twisting a little against the vacuum-sealed joint of meat. he notices the damp of her hand is mildy affecting the phone. she says she's sitting on the kitchen counter, ready to do it again. he thinks he has never heard one with an orphaned permanence in her voice, waiting so remarkably for him to get guessing. he hesitates and strides to his couch, inhaling once and taking off his clothes silently. "I can feel your cock," she rolls her voice, as he makes it to the middle of the *Wheel of Fortune.* he recloses his eyes until the sound of sucking takes on a sharper feel, like the world map rolling to the top of the blackboard with a violent snap, reappearing as if trickling sweet corrections. she sighs heavily as he fishes out a story on Hollywood divorce rates and throws it in to the infrequently used garbage can. she moans while he takes his eraser to miniaturize his signature on his diary cover in to an invisible finish. he begins to incline his hips towards his choice of a "l," but the letter remains unturned. he feels like someone is sanding his voice away, as his hearing slows to her unusually pressured "n," and he readies himself to handle seeing the completed word. sinking in to a compensatory lag as the blink of his cum appears on the screen on Vanna's imitative lips. he quickly dabs another coat of cologne on a pile of unsent envelopes. he pulls his zipper back and hangs up, before turning to erase the sub-celebrity tape he has made, still sure her voice is floating gently and tightly in at him, going everywhere he can't bare to be.

Inmate

she declares she is just un-where and a ducty day, just soiling the gusset of control hose. that it's wormed away from her coxa and unenlargeably curled at her natal cleft. to the unpacking plank of ladder-backs. holding her nose at the cerumen, where the black colloidal bristles were bitten in foreshortened visits. grisaille sere, missing the eustachial itch's planting of pilonidal drainage with old sfumatrice's peel of the moried tiered skirt the tsessbe's coat's dulled dacquoise piping trails with the last part of the syringing. fixed on the horizontality in the stanley cell, as she spreads the single blanket, with the tonsillar warp of lanan wool inseams. cricoidal in the bunched motionlessness without the hefting of signed letting-to-know

conincidentally, striding to the bathroom to damp her face from savasana, her hands wracked from the anjali press. taking the vending of panty liner lone from the shootout. laying it flat, beetling backwards with the array of small cross-body bags from its stain that she wipes gently. a ramune bolus pillared a distance from the frenziedly turning-in cavity at the back of her throat. hypocarbic, her darting finger on the prosom she took, reflected in graffitied villi in the mirror. appearing to be the same distance, to the side as in front, the large matzo meal ball, from which everyone was to whittle an acceptable scoop. the shaoxing rice wine dashed on moo shoo pancake already at her pharynx, an allodynia as she hooks the zakkaya plastio strip

around her wrist. a flakey drop from the ear spoon on it, as she tries to edge the appurtenant countenance up. thatched brows sheltering more in waiting for the share taxi. the girl picking the imipramin fused where the akoya post found falling from one of the fans of longhorn hair. to violaceous whiskered jeans, plumped to anatomical fullness on bird-brittle shaped balloons. in the heat of 300°F ovens, a sandblasting crawling it up, over, under and through the taction of keloidally re-piercing it muonic, with the rousts of their hands darely touching, warming it, as he's kept unapprised as it's smeared on them. lighted menbo unspooling maroilles-like on the transept of a chest's oblong sticker, faledom. swallowing sparringly at some heard unhelped over kerbs

---

mori, refers to a style in Japan starting round 2006, called so as the look involves softened, natural, woodsy qualities. Basic to the style, layered long and tiered skirts, classic floral prints, small cross-body bags, scarves and stoles

allodynia, refers to a pain due to a stimulus which does not normally evoke pain. This other power-like process can be either thermal or mechanical

zakkaya, refers to knick-knack stores, related to mori girl interests

menbo, a variety of q-tips in Japan, some sticky, some with black tips and there's a lighted ear pick, items that are involved in ear wax fetishism

Sisters

letting herself hold the key, pulling the loop from the mousseux
of the barbamama keychain. the plastoy filing back to bombous
as she reaches near the letters splayed advertising and wig labels.
partly gathered in a bunch as her tips trail for the de-sil and yak
milk. looping to the old shrigley for sale button incised at a line
on a panty's sticking waist which she shakily gestures, dingling
the hatch's re-shuffle of envelopes. tilting to the lashful salacity
of the small blindworm's batting of eyelids, with a tabular stone
shrugged slowly, the herkimer's opposing centre facets snagged
with one of the smooth ventral scales. managing to commove off
lint-like, to open the screen door. bestride for a moment the sharp
knuckled twigs, small pebbles with the things that hurt zipper pull

kunckle clasped in toeing from the simple physalis garland, sitting
the carrot barfi on the couch, as she in slovenly urgency apologies
the class ran late, while flinging the punchlike tabi's stall cross the
closing door from the dishevelled bed –to prime the saltopus, while
on about a sort of tergiversation, the odor of toulene, as she stuffs
the faint musky smell of shiroan on the mens' tank, which bulges
in resistivity from the torn club chair. she drapes her legs over the
back of it, lappet hair to the hollowed-out balls per uzbek odango.
in difficulty raising the footrest with the mirthness with the hair's
onsets. the lipoatrophy that needs doing for the next. quainks of a
flanker lid's himalayan tea, as she rotates a leg from it, at where a
kancho will start. not hearing a call to jap-hah gann fong, setulae

---

de-sil, tibetan rice pudding made from broken rice, perceived as the low-
    est grade of rice, which is ideal for creating a thicker, smoother texture
herkimer, a term for the double-terminated quartz crystals, found in the

Herkimer area in New York, known for their good clarity

tergiversation, evasion of clear-cut expressions or straightforward action

shiroan, substance made from lima or navy beans in to a white bean paste

kancho, prank performed by clasping the hands together so the index
fingers are pointing out and attempting to insert them into someone's
anal region

odango, refers to double or pigtail bun styles in Japan

jap-hah gann fong, clean your room in Cantonese

An Mo

a pu pu chi playing on the tsuzimi, not that his gryposised tips actually touch, with routing of his thumb's exostosis snagged on the shuffle of hopsack tweed coat, cut as a cape. revealing kashakas around the neck's soft clack, re-fastening the plastic holder for kuai-ji. not inserting a loonie, along with the canto-jingles, at joey's pride in your eyes, wai ngo goi seh har boon sung. the staggering to the supernal of schwarzkopf osis paste, left unopened. with a small amount lodged in the slender, near like avascularity of his hands poised near the frisyr punkabilly style. not raking it through, specks falling on it like spicules of the sun's chromosphere, moving off from the bracketed crown. ducking straight to the lavatory, beneath the short stairs, by the rush of a lukewarmadilling tap, fashioning a kind of splint with his belt to follow soon to the touches of toilet papers, as if along

golden apple narguilés. hearing a screech of foot-basin, his head lowered to where the glint of teeth pressed. it's delayed with his left black sesame panna cotta inverted with the zhi mu seedlings decocting, like the wode spray he dabs from the curettement just cropped. sensing the brandish misshapement of the rope flag on the leg, in untying the miniskirt and overall. the sentential pause of petrissage as he returns to talk, not more then yatbaak pounds of shui mai dough. as he pushes through valsavar exhalations of his own, gripping the mug tightly with clary sage iridium on the tranverse ligament along the inside of his wrist. turning away as to not let show the filling, the futtering with the taked-to stack of seitan dumplings. just before refilling the circulatory smoothy he has made in the bowl. in the mumbles for service complet, as she backs away, a tremor laying wrappers, saltatory double thickness

---

an mo, massage in Cantonese

tsuzimi, a Japanese drum, struck with the tips of the fingers

kuai-zi, chop-sticks

wai ngo goi seh har boon sung, means you changed your life for me. It's a lyric from the Joey Yung song "My Pride." She is a canto-op star perceived to be perhaps gay herself or at least sensitive in some of her music to queer concerns

zhi mu, herb used to clear heat, moisten dryness

yatbaak, a hundred (Cantonese)

Step By Step

taking steps slowly, around the gradual field of fitted shirts by the duffel, she takes the scarf tucked in the zip exterior pocket. the rendered change end is swoopy with the shoe inserts she wrote. the deui-mèh-jyuh with the whole length of his shoes that are abrading more acutely on the outsides as he approaches with the camera in his hands, as she leans inadvertently at the nearest wall, her hand on the rewind switch of the petite black slim. the counter retarded at marking a duration before the sacre de printemps, between the ivied hospital walls, pressing the telescope at the bedspread drawn over the pillow clumsier, seemed emptier than the walking of the stretcher, as she trotted close behind and they had to let go of the fifties cupped bra patched across the soaked duchesse satin lining at where the epispadias, runs nearly diagonal on a stretched leg, knocking the empty

styrofoam of ramen. patting the crenature of bite marks around the rim, with still a notable hint of katsuo. like from a kotteri as her film counter aflutters to a stop, as the padded siracha on the moyashi sprouts is spat in the already soiled handkerchief. lips sternly compressed on a nexium while the small spits continue, thickened like dragée gum. as his spoon retracts, taking the can opener he starts to use in no wider, than what is is lodged further down his chest. around the interventrical septum, skin stretched like a calamansi palet. as he nods at the wheeled fujitsu suited trying to take both legs off from densely pleated baggy trousers. whilst recorded snores diminishing, the coffee coloured plush paws taking off the spunbond shoe covers, its heavy duty plastic on the bottom tearing with the clumsily extemporized foldout bed. catching a fulgidity at the

camera nose spots alternating from where its fur marginally depressed between the eyes to the nose end and at where the outer vestment little by little proliferous. as it shuffles closer to where she felt for the small stick of paper placed on the telephone with the pinellia. in the leading tail of spoon in a circular waltz around the rasalhague opening trotted close behind. in his I want you to do so much so fast, with a lens set at wider angles, stepping over the recalcitrant pieces of broken cup, while her hair wisped not grown long enough for pig-tails is crossed over the uneven saucer's dribble. how urgently the teensy bit of colour restored by the jigger, when she sucked it through a straw, leading an ethanoled finger to the open hole. the liquid suspended over the half torn heap of pop-up spires and flagpoles with the sinai mag. infixes quivering again

---

katsuo, skipjack tuna in Japan

deui-m̀h-jyuh, I'm sorry

fujitsu, a bear robot developed with 300 different responses, with supposed capacity to read human expressions, deployed in elderly and other ailing situations

Loth

walking along boards covering hospitalic wefts of her hair with paving rice, the effort hunching, pulling the round brass doorplate, where the old foxed mirror is fitted, spine out by the quiet warps of nitro dur patches, the nudge of the teva-gabapentin bottle jiggeting, as she pulls the mock up with graver hands, with the strip poker chocolate game wheel falling. a slowed effort to spin the wheel, as it points to the slot emptied, when after the bite of a hard centre, the unseating of a printed polyester filled skirt, to the l'emmerdeuse to take something clsc off. the long strided carrying back of the harapan, so spottily sallowed with dit da jow and peroxide. her muscled rigidity starting with the sudden tow of her pearls, looped around her back, as her chest-side affrayed, releasing crepitant rales with the scuffed forking her pallor with the chipped stale-centred last and the corresponding need put something on. the flicker of anger, letting fall the tin's list of fairly simple ingredients, with its capital letters reading "THIS IS AN ADULT PRODUCT," her mind clearing

not fast enough, bestrode a phantosmia in the restless surroundings' with the rolling out of basi apple, the splutter of bagged out kampyo makis, titivates headrest in the refractory block. by the single barred window, the squeezed image of pinked kanas lake, beneath the nonprecipitating stratiform clouds, that'll run along the wall. the low-lying rosy color, as she wraps her hair up with the tuvan jaw harp, as parting teeth goes closer to her occiput, much as bandied legs manipulable notices an exaggerated languor, tipping each side of her not quite sedulous squirt over wall-eyeing repetitive kargyraa motion. enough daylight, the shadow of the largactil on the pallet, making off to the floor's radiant in-slab. clanking in the depradation of her feet moved closer to the slashed binding, holding it closed. the idling swish in the press to see it again, just set to be seen more at grated pvc pipe. cleaving her apothecial hackling of loth hands on glassed-in shoulders, so fleet the last's steadying to increase holdspace, mid the hefty barge of cracks slewed unrecapturably

---

dit da jow, popular pungent liniment sold to heal external damage such as bruises or sore muscles

kanas, China's deepest freshwater lake, described by some as "God's palette" because of its rich variety of colors. When the water is clear, you can see a blue and green lake; underneath the thin clouds, Kanas Lake is pink; and when it is overcast, the lake is blue and grey.

kampyo, cooked gourd, the strips resembling heavy twine

kargyraa, a deeper sounding style of Tuvan throat singing

Chousing

seen and vanished, the hny scratched in the bird-in-hand compact –the laterocollis of its tail base, where the propecia was accommodated, conforming to the overripe sea buckthorn, near rancid on platysma creased intakeness of her peaked lapel. she takes the hazardous sour wrappers from the ruffle cravat placket, flattened and wrapped in to a gaiter. a few hours after the amped lemon, the tissue around the negligible torus on the roof of her mouth still sore. to a glass tipping its acid phosphate, not having to fake a sour countenance. removing the uv ball lodged with a risorius irradiating from a subnotebook, the whipperwills' whistly calls going quieter, as imposingly emptied prie-dieu placed in front of the neon gen for short tapestry. preceded by the strand of pearls with the feminine, asplash on the spot long bereft of prayers. with its sucking its thumb, she sees how the fur is loosened about its hand, like a bistered filling. like pulling the collected of what's not caught up in the suckle, the natal teeth, implosive in being found. imperfectly dried with a finger cot, as she rolls her cheeks dropping start below her jaw line. rhythmic sough of its marmit-parts, past the mecha figures

recovering from the so called "second impact," which annihilated half of the world's population. binaural, she can't complete the tendency to describe handrolled unload on ischaemian embrace in ryōan-ji park, where toyed footfall leaves thoracic tussle, heard from mown venusaur rugosity. the bud on its back has since bloomed into the large red flower, supported on a trunk like that of a palm tree, at a pause at the ofuro. from dozens of corners, she can't find her orgel. barely at anamnesis, sliding down it, she senses puchi-barks at the top of her thighs' impersonation of packthread working up from shins, she kneels down to disused water –her arches feel lifted, teetering and inclining the soap on to wambling blastoise, swerves a garotte floating tetanic, when the lisianthic aril stain with his suspender hose is reeled down in to two donuts, with the perservation at her clenched pterygoid triangle. with the unlocking of brachiales, the push again to his shoulder and a slow-goes' desquamate. clutches candy lunules, as he tries to tighten by degrees around her neck. jaggedly, his glabellar maeandra is lifted, the plashing of his orgulous unsaid, her epiglottises' nuguishin, sheu-n stiffed

---

ofuro, Japanese bath tub

orgel, a pull-cord 3-minute music box used by women to keep track of timings for different parts of their bath routines.

puchi, refers to Puchi Puchi virtual bubble wrap toy

blastoise, a bipedal tortoise with a shell that has two jutting water cannons

maeandra, a genus of brain corals

nuguishi, crumpled paper strewn around lovers in shunga, indicating lovemaking has taken place

sheu-n, sour in Cantonese

Woolies

counting the tide of segmental achromicus from where the jikitabi hase lifted for the non skid, non constrictive sock. her right foot over her right leg begins to fall asleep, with the allowed weight onto the woodier cast of the trad milky tennis ball, inside the outer hip bone under her nates. held at the noted area of added soreness, where it's glögg tableting. its headiness softened in the profit diaper's gathered slim crotch. the sediment not sawn in the mornings, while it grows more vandaceous and inspissated, her face never flickered at it over the week, except at the je n'en peux plus, in quelling the rot of onc of the leathers arranged in the accompanying chairs. sitting beside a benignly wheezing older basker. while she alone gazes out across the terraces at the sky's sole cumulus congestus. as the crisp, sharp edges of its summit softens, at barely where it's settled at the carpopedal spasm and unviewing the formspring api key pressed, the answer me when did you last suck back the scratchiest crocodile clunge, as even with the femoral nerve block, the purpura lambs pride brushes against her

in bulkish spats. it's adjustable side buckle system loosened on slight lipedema. as they all piled, ratios of the acinetobacter infested workers clothes in off-tusk in bins, with the cartoon like paper backings of unopened gumis. watching as it took the better part of eight minutes to peel the gumi unko from its plastic mold. at which it left brown markings, similar to snail excretion going unintentionally on the appearedness of the resting soundly form. the evening's phugoidic routes continuing with the trudged in family formations, unfastening pork lung soup's mixing with post-nasal drip, as the women patients growing more excitable with the pingueculae flashed, with her last move wiping the outer orbits of her alpaca lace yarn stretched across her face's sudden start to an honesty's ho sai li, whilst more and more, she pulled the glassine envelopes with the perfins she made with the omorashic preparation of shadows of things out of place. looking to their very wearing of it, with genuflecting conferring. going amissed in the overlying shawl, where it was rived in unanimity of disappointment, the oliguric bow buey of munt

---

jikitabi hase, product that makes the jikatabi (tabi boots) wider for a better fit. Simply attach it to your jikatabi and you've added up to 5 cm.

crocodile clunge, a vagina that is a crocodile's mouth and takes up the entirety of the lower body. The term originates from a movie called "Tokyo Gore Police" featuring a girl who actually has a crocodile clunge

unko, shit or poop in Japanese

ho sai li, dangerous in Cantonese

omorashi, fetish subculture recognized predominantly in Japan in which participants experience arousal from having a full bladder or a sexual attraction to someone else experiencing the feeling of a full bladder

bow buey, preciousness (Cantonese)

munt, rare slang expression, referring to the relatively fresh, but slightly rotted gash of a female corpse, ready to have the bodily fluids gushing out of it into a munter's mouth. Best served ice-cold.

Means, Ends

if he hears her, he does not reply in choking down the hairy crab leg since it's shelled, he focuses on the corners of the separé with every turn out of range. there's a bearing of his fingers managing to locate the hot oshibori towel, looped around the bagging of the ringo-chan urging the cropped knife, voiding the adductor attached to a scallop when a man with a removed jacket of grody tuftiness sits, grabbing a strip of jinhua ham to a thinly generous smile in the "is that her?" flecking her vasti before she's tugged up by the halter necked collar in an rnc, twined between her father's digits. with a knashing of the car-park of a mouth, she's halting on a lippy obrotund like enthalpy

waking cramped, she sees a room with a motorized perforated metal shutter downwardly pivoting. a familiar twitch is camptodactylic as he jerks the plastic finger, while blastula of poo soars on the screen the other mishandling a pot of mac purple shower to create the look of bruising caused by forcible restraint. she's about to scream "no" until her father adds covering hands, to where he slapped his across her face. a chipped houndstooth check nail tip is pressed where the abrasion to remove the assailant's hands are placed. after a slinged photo, a facecloth is extended with a sewn on doll. exuding m'gois during registering the wetness already on the eyelet edged petticoat

---

m'goi, thank you in Cantonese, said for receiving service

Unikelihood

going down the stairs, he sees them at the starting easing, all but coming, as he waggles the strada bianca from the sole of the chukka boot, while it issues a hint of regolithic moonlight, by the pot of galanthus by the front door. heart-shaped green blotches on each of its several inner petals start to sway, at just about the prong of a tight saffron bud. its emerging sighs with his rumbly emollience of thieved unkaikaku water, amid such leaves that have died back. oleophobicity of herring-udon with a touch of inside pocket, of out of pocket, in views of a low light in the apartment, with the spald pipping near the pailou's base, affixed sufficiently not upright, with the leaving of graffittied door open, while it still slides shut. key dropped

on the landing, as he watches the single passing of the luna nera of a bertha collar. an overcoat with the irremovable lining's summary of the matsuzaka stain, from the hastened valving of orechiette removed in the caf. while still sensing hooked glochidia on each of the valve margins pendant. its rhodium plated silver and red gold, hooked on the always returned to flat spots on the anterior of his head, that had improvement without the doc band, that he kept pulling off, with the wolffia he washed off, that kept growing on the surfaces of his dunked uniform. after school, the brushing off of the rootless ovals, in a sort of gua sha extravasation, palpating the pulses below his waist, where he tucked the ero guro crania. with an externity of another bandage extended off

hearing muffled ring, he turns and straightens to the slantier check marks on it against the door. its repetitive pitches as he takes to a re-grip the recentest kuih. its koshian hastate to an arch, as he doesn't take it's dissimilar, that it's fallen, like in somebody's plated jacket's collar. with the squature to the key, in still following his dai ga jeer, her head unlifted at some indistinct areas on the stairs with feigned indecision. along the sidelines of sock toppers, not up on the wind-downing of knocks, his previously unlined brow turns the tv dial down low, while there's the tapping of footsteps, he's shown the old buttons had snapped on a kodona blouse. an unsounded alarm, the de-verging, while the nanchatte seifuku laughter fades. not looking around the door's kanzashi

matsuzaka, refers to cuts of beef from the black tajima, considered a delicacy

gua sha, a Chinese massage that involves repeated pressurized strokes on skin that may result in blemishing

dai ga jeer, big sister in Cantonese

kodona, the boys' solution to the popular Japanese "Lolita" fashion. It involves wearing a style similar to what Victorian boys wore

nanchatte seifuku, literally translated as "fake uniform" a kind of fashion that is increasingly popular with girls in Tokyo

Toky seifuku, refers to types of everyday uniforms, not belonging to a school or institution, often customized by their owners

kanzashi, a craft beginning with squares of fabric, folded in to dimensional petals to assemble myriad flower designs

Detection

toying with the borsone zip top, held together by a lesser peg at its base
confused why it appears to stop along mt huangshan's bryophytal mats.
trying to adjust to the jolt of the dehiscence of the underfeets' hs tracts,
in her bit t-strap sandals. unlike the anatomic anti-microbial footbeds of
the other hikers, starting another ridge hike before going down, while a
stray ootoro piece is pushed in to the fallen bread boule, she tears, while
a lot of its hollow crust vaults to the bucket with the sweat tops slapped.
dropping the anti fog visor over the wave-back protector, slipped out of
the elasticated corduroy inserts on the dainese under-sleeve's perspired
senmaizuke scent like ouverts, as she arches out the lordotic curve with
the shogoin turnip's nigh eight inch diameter globe being lodged, with
slowing of her arms, like hollow stalks away from its by flashes, by the
ropeway that was open when she's down to it. a ride from the cable car
down, just before the sign at the station warned of dangerous bail force

winds. taking gulps of huo shan that holds a sapor of the yingke glair at
the start with a sweet carryover in the swallowing. in casting of her lips
to the rim, peering back at the moderately steep trail, with switchbacks
through pine forest where it's stalled. batting it up in the air, catching it
again like an extrusion of smooth yarn. slowly rolling it, as in pretense
of losing it utterly. the photographer pointing through the rain, at where
the trail is much rougher, chains at several points along it. while it halts
by a sheer dropoff, where's a leaning to tuck behind ears a sycee of rat
hair piece. to the strain of con te partiro, a mudcaked finger trails to the
surface of the tea, to her pink slip's diddlining against a protracted run.
noticing the cupping of hands over ears, abreast her by-passing of arms,
with the torn piece of veil held on to opposite elbows, in remanding the
stop in the walk over. exponence of distrust to a desisted simper, as she
raises it against the setting steps, to sunkibilical beats, sniffles snarfling

senmaizuke, the noted pickle of Kyoto is made from turnip, salt-pickled for
  up to a month with konbu (a seaweed), mirin or sugar, and chili peppers
huo shan, yellow tea in Cantonese
con te partiro, a phrase of with you I will go, that's also an Italian classical
  crossover tune written by Francesco Sartori
diddl, a cartoon white jumping mouse created by Thomas Goletz
sunki-zuke, made using the leafy tops of red beets and is unusual that the
  process requires no salt, fermented in natural lactic acid bacteria

Under Try

uncertain near the black field to the tail-tip, hind legs kicking against her heel in to one-eyed sursumduction at the knife magnet, from the dongpo pork jus' burnt waxed form. cooling in the biopolymer gel, its about two mm of meat running horizontally across the fat that's five cm high at end to end, pivoting the hau diao yellow wine slightly, with the glance at the count down on the timer, already started from four hours. as she starts to score its skin with parallel slits, repeating in a perpendicular direction in the fixaprene mitts, that'd help the top layer of fat render off. even as the pair built resistant to stains and five hundred degrees, she wrists the right one off, to an itching and slight vesiculation. like a wrist tendinopathy in the bared other that dropped it in the wok. while removing it, the moisture leaches out of it as it caramelizes. the weight of the splitting of it, near the fridge's pod of lotus plumules near the bottom. half turning to the strings of lights, the adding of another 30 feet to allow for the pitch of some roof,

leaving it set aside when all its sides have sealed, ungripping the heaviest based pot in the thickly lined sweatshirt sleeves. with the colour changing led stars beginning to flash red, then like a shadow-dyed powder blue, not to an acuity of green as a long-tailed tit tats at her finger along a few faux carriage lamps, the motion sensors and their solar-powered path spotlights they recently put in at the half of the block. while a finger-thumb rub feels like the part dirt and half buttered popcorn jelly nacelle on a bare bulb, she keeps from her straitened days. rolled axially by the scotchgarded thelman skirt, pulling the tiers up, as the dwarf juniper reveals a girl by the passed out first alc leather military jacket, her cigarette jeans nudged aside, as the purse fallen is gone through. in the staggering in, pushing the men's pocky, studded in feuillatine in gold-leaf. depressing it from her lower lip, a pause lunging from the adipose chunk unplaced in the pot. halfway backed down the stairs, the half turning to the zhu tou, without facing an esemplastic nod

at the bottom

dongpo pork, a slow braised fatty pork belly named after a Song dynasty poet,
zhu tou, literally meaning "pig head," or moron

Out of Sight

sunlight peers through the lightly shirred valance scalloped across, overseeing the generality of light at it barely ½ diameter, its culm internodes beginning to bulge. its ten inch cut piece, unsecuring from the rest of them in the decorative rock, as she pulls the fleece blanket with "yum gong" across her head, which's not thrown back as excessively drowsily. transparencies of the line of pet cans, get set against the highering relief of linked spirals of leiwen cloud, thunderous with the brontide of the guang, dropping with her groping for the missed taoties. projecting her elbow, the spouted vessel's lid like a toothy bottle-horned dragon is fumbled unopened on the cervalign pillow. feeled first at its indented center in lifting in partly back, its vaulted hinge pressing to the side of her throbbing head with its okonomiyaki-width blur of swirling petals, her last night's face with the chu-hai she drank like mirroring just her glassy-eyedness on a vinyl disc, raised quickly over the embrasure, between the clapping and stagy rejoicing. a sweatied palm's sleeve design incorporating a spider's web, with her hands pedimented at

the elbow joint, forming the centre like Cissé's. while the aseities of it, at a flight below to the lanai balcony, the nihon-shu she passes on, shifting to unsightliness dose, like the kind when it's already hard to face it moreover. toward a panel van parked on its rear tires, while its front goes resting, against the corner of the vivil tea jutting. the stray maxillipeds she tries to ease from her ankle's plantar flexion, not readily outstretched as an arm glides with rearward drafts in the driver's seat. the arm is not exactly graceful as she peruses her similar lanterned sleeve elytraly. she pockets the retraded phone that rings, to her quick pickup to a voice-mail, left to herself nearly two hours back. slow vesicular tones identified with the strode to the curb, the stopping for mei jia wu as the holden was late. she headed away from the watching them go, gaining on the teaching of english in a third-storeyed class, numbering a dog's bark before noticing what kleenex forming cylindrical waggles from the passenger side. wistfully caespitose, resurveying the missed opportunities that crowded and the obvulate stria to the other, who's always at the same moment

yum gong, pity

guang, a traditional spouted ritual wine vessel

taotie, a motif commonly found on ritual bronze vessels from the Shang dynasty. The design typically involves a zoomorphic monster mask, described as being frontal, bilaterally symmetrical, with a pair of raised eyes and typically no lower jaw area

okonomiyaki, a savoury pancake containing a variety of ingredients. The name refers to the word okonomi, meaning "what you like or want," while yaki means "cooked."

mei jia wu, a Chinese tea that has a light nutty aroma, smells of fresh leaves, very smooth taste

Low-Budging

rising at 6 pm all-scanning to the stocked fridge's brocciu, too much of it olent. even if it was just spooned with the dripping off of shapes corvined at the finial's embedded heart. as it drips from the handle like a coal chute, the patina adhoc by the hardscrabble whisper of his lashes, balling his fists at the yeasty gloam at his headstall. stopping the tear, breathed frayedly on the ptomaine pouring from the bag of lamb mince, in his unrolling it overly along their stewing necks. the catholicity of it moulded in the waxed paper stein over his mussed barbae. re-forming swing which claps a jone's bottle in two second cobbing of pattered glass, after closing the door behind him,

by the brief desistance from the ear-hurting call, wong ji. with the briefcase on his knees, the penlight from his wide tailored pant rotating at his coxae's baconnaise. as he wipes the sucralose, a little felon on the streak near dartoic of rectangular a4 pad. a snaking touch assessing the glued edge's muculence apoke from the bumpy side margin. as he ungainily ridges the mmmattempts at appeals of pathmnemonic, as the lines like treman falls appears on a ripped page, screeched as the compressed membrane of a terry robe is bent out while his clearance coming through. the amousing of his collar stays removed, nicht wahr is sat back. the sprig of sowbug collapsed inwards prods his foot unshod,

as he halts in a stomp and desultorily cranks his supporting leg, just capping the knee. sickling the chloracne with his fingers, pushing portions of his belly at the dupled shoved tane-koji. enshrouding the rueing erection with the nukazuke left for several weeks. with the distant brakelights of eyes on her dimples, just deep enough to fit his butte, surbating it from the rear to bellowing the straight-sided pot, still with the mustered duckboard whilom. while his cervicis is lain, ahung backward off the couch. the beginning of the "ahhh" sound in the technique like before, using every effort with knees pigeoned inward, thickly tortile haunching to force the sonance of a cry, expirating with last of iri-nuka bids, for their while

brocciu, a whey cheese produced from sheep milk or goat milk

wong ji, prince (Cantonese)

tane-koji, a type of starter spore preparation used in the making of miso

nukazuke, a type of cucumber made by flavoring it in a pickling mixture of nuka, kelp, dried chilis, etc. and had after burial for several months

iri-nuka, toasted rice bran used in the preparation of nukazuke

Come Off

[Click.] she enters the lobby, by a long trestle table where going around the side of the low rise sofa by the breakfasted laid for one, gently bringing the other layer of the egg mixture, raised from the blown forwards batch as its stops to set the odori-ebi, along a pegasid amulet, while burgeoning for the opening of the hotel room, unreaching its corridor's gemütlichkeit of putto, overlooking the reheated coffee plied, it occuring to vary the ripped seamed tussle of eschewed pikelet, while it's unpacked adjacent to her along with a ring-back tone. a bit of slapple in his cernuous saying it may be suitable for a night or two. a couple of minutes later, the angling of her slightly pebbled cheek averted from the sidled airtime detail isn't captured, precluded during the daybed's suppositious testing, teetering his buttocks over the spessartite quilting. as he closes in on the brocade cushion near one end, with the arare lodged, she lolls pressing the cushion at the foot-end without any particular reaction as he mumbles it'll be more then satisfactory. a shift in her gaze in

[Cick.] attempt at comity, while her fingertips grows chillier as he pats the marram near her digitation. staring across furlongs of carpet to the bar, as he retains the receipt from the maitre d excusing, despite their best efforts as he raises his outturned hands to shoulder height, bowing his head while she asks if he's arrived yet. shaking his head, she sags on the quilting with undissimulated muttering, if he will recognize her and how delayed it'll be as he whuffles her thin shoulder blades, against his supporting hand when she leans, ranging from face to entering face. behind the porter, the look at her, in a hiding wrench of the serrated batiste, pulled from the tin ex-votos' catflaps, throbbing the packet of istara cheese crackers, the best she's to do. in glancing back to the hallway's wadded paper over the brown-grey waste of melted snow, ensuite handouts counterbalancing ribolittas of hydroceles in her lower lenses, catching their fringing of pop-it beads. the charlie tuna camera's flashcubes wavering, to the static posing, all thread-jammed keshi

odori-ebi, dancing shrimp, so named because they are eaten alive

arare, type of bite-sized Japanese cracker made from glutinous rice, associated with luck

keshi, small, non-nucleated pearl, commonly formed as by-product of pearl cultivation, also known as poppy seed pearl

Increscence

the most unexpected gift, the fluttered graphic print of varied sized skulls pulled out from her coldly gyrated neck that falls on it's background blue, graphing a sky blown clean of d'orange verte clouds. the concentré below the agretti knotting under her chin as she wanders a little way off, from the keeping up of wrapping in a sheltered spot. finds it hard to keep going with the greens cooking, giving off a sulphur-dirt scent. like in the same 0.8 mms as vermicelli, yet around her nuchal rigidity. some whimzy deco paper over her arching brows, lifted high like croquet hoops, in standing out by the side of the window's sharpness of a rotated chioggia beet, as she glanced then to the candy cane stripes on the bath shake. scanning the sloping concrete step and its three tier false front of paintless clapboard, while the strawberry tone at the shake's top is placed against her cheek, feeling coarser as she pushes it back from her spiny strands. watching the hand-lettered sign below new asia, pasted up between aged advertisements with pyramids of fried, twisted sanzi

as the rends of the papery skins of cipollini onions are limped at the window, like from a one-room ell. the brushing of the fizzling of the sandalwood level bumping her hand up and down along the back, as she compresses the tighter psoas muscles on his right, refusing to go supine. with his legs spreading like scissors against the sliding pane, he tries to control his head from moving, in the sliding side to side of the grimed and just cracked plate-glass window, its adhesive tape being mended from the inside, as she catches the clench in his jaws, at titian hair cropped in a bowl cut, as she applied histoacryl blued glue to the back of her head shaved, decumbent, the ruby stems of warnstorf moss, when grown in shade. it's not as difficult, the waivering, having wanted, with reaching a hand and the hold of the base of the thumb to the side of the cue-v, that's extended back on the nakashima table. down-playing her obstruant pain conspecific with the quavering of the reQall widget and the near some edging to ho paura, as she shifts his cupped ear superjacent to it, the going in glumes,

awnless

Remotely

undrowsily, the hiss of rain heard in her sitting at the table, her hands raising by the teacher's desktop. seeing the icons of the students on the board at the top in their pleated necklines, one with a prescott plaid cape, the other encircled with a floral bib necklace, quieted in the wait of a drive back, the snow starting again in the while too cold for them to stay put, as one edged her feet from the sill, taking up a guitar against her coat. its stiffened bellows resisting as the other gestures in the radio active trefoil interpreted as a miscommand by the software, in this case a new window on the tipped up on one leg over the calaveras skull fanned pelvic rocking form. the head and shoulders on the sitting room floor, in the wriggle of mayreau long sleeve cowl, of its year of the rabbit amigurumi's bluntly dangling bunnies with portholes, as they're bumped by noisier gusts of veldt-lasted crepe soles, protecting from electric shock. the flurry of smart phone carrying blare of go eat shit or die, as the goddamn of one from the remained seated is called for a small ski-jump nose, during the budget committee's meeting. as she feels the left overed small crochet basket for the pyogenic button to be in, with the quick quit of the few wailing notes of the scoffed instrument. unwatching the panted perma poxing like assthmatic babies. she stops by the worn trooling banners in the wind

ripped broom racket, dapping abreast the well-balanced small tack hammer with the unfinished toast of coconut-egg jam grilled with butter. the midsyllable crest of it on her nepwimper, drawn as it's with her own lashes with them, in brushing the rheum resulting in having an even lesser amount than the semied-permanent extensions. its faux snake-skin pressed leather strip with dysthymic sob, caught on the knit headphone cozy pattern between her fainting scissor hold of the note of don't know what's going to happen after this eviction. desisting the drawing of a field, zoomed out from their pulling the ometosandon baby doll's spraddle, towards the top of the uterus, which helps to prevent pressure from constricting its umbilical cord. in her declinating the unclaimed deposit can from their path, to the low-pitched hum of her stretch bracelet's caespitose on the speaker fabric of honeycomb design to add nodes, the ways each of them pulled the jaai mihn by the counter, whilst out of the hisses of traffic and ceaseless lurching of work, the contracter begins to carry out plan on property that has not been empty, her stiff-legged right dragged behind a left that is backing away with the tarnished spoon's kwan kung gods, fringed by post-christimas bulbs. depurates guan dao before an obvoluting orderliness, to the fitting it in along the frühstückic others

---

omotesandō, a famous shopping district, termed Tokyo's Champs-Élysées, with kiddyland
jaai mihn, vegetarian, plain noodles
kwan kung, general in Chinese history, titled god of war, known for his defence of politicians, businessmen, and the armed forces
guan dao, Chinese pole weapon

Cloakness

the tip of the hope and peace cigarette misdirected beside her forearm's kebori mole, close to the uniform surface of the xanthous crust with the rolled back plum border. the replica much like what wrenched under an antique long cotton stocking from the kestner. finding she's unstared at as she turns up the alley to their yard, to scrutinize where the apron clip was held to raise the dishcloth, to catch the healing burn scar, about the diameter of a round 70 mm stub. deliberately penning where it ached in small coils near her asis, as the hands laid to both palpably feel them on the thin-shanked re-clasp of the guilinggao, that spills on the chiu chow dumpling's transparent skin. a small tarmac darkening in the collecting the plastic utensils, half seating to part the banana leaves with the salted egg yoke. its surface cleared of the mushed mung, goes icy to the touch as its presumed handled between the bunched up tea towel, refraining as one of the gauyou's yolks is tubed in the busby end of the toy marchman

in the turning to the kitchen, by the smoked-in-all-the-time office, a faint quivering to the clutched views along its drag oak floor. in heading to the opaque glass screen bordering the living room, where she crouches in the picking up the drum major's white hat. minus its plume, she deflexes it at the surface, averting her eyes from its blood-red scour, toward the rest of the washing-up. formlessly awaiting reuse, the parping of the trunks from the sat on edge of an armchair, a daunted trailing of a hoarse cry for more green works liquid. with the gloved fingers deployment of the waffle dish towel left aside, for the check patterned rag. in grappling the lodged ashes, along the itch of a leg band's moisture-wick, she gets to the glen urquhart patterned flap, hanging down the busby, which was less bulky when it was

reached backward in her throat. an arrhythmia to her vocalic tremor, as she passes it suggestured to the bonzoed-ash tray. by arching of a support-sling blouson, asking if it was a good time last night, tobacco columns' impaction

---

kebori, the tattooing of fine lines or hair on tattooed forms

guilinggao, the black herbal jelly with a sharp bitterness, made of powdered turtle shell and china roots, thought to combat cancer and improve the complexion

gauyou, the double-yolked salted duck egg, considered rare, with a yolk, blood-red in colour–they were used as tribute to some emperors

Desorption

as she orders him the ma tei gow, she shifts the shoulder sling that keeps the noppera-bō tight to her side. a brisk snort having her stretching for a paper napkin, applying it lightly, at an angle from the rubberiness of the mucosa before. it falls, her eyes tipping from the diffusivity and pausing through the openwork spandrel under the s-shaped armrest. she wriggles on the zitan chair, trying to identify it, like stabilized on the haphazardly tied layers at the waist. watching as it's coated in a ti leaf. gently pressed it before turning it over on to the wipeable table cover. his cap pulled low his hand on a flush paper bag by the table, as he begins depilling the cod milt of the miyoga sliver, turning the spongy mass like a girolle, while in

a riffle, her palprebal lines have stayed dry, while disconjugate in a once over the slight tissue, after the recent demanded extraction. insubstantial, thermals of the metrorrhagia, the leachate by the ginch gonch's contrast trim. basking jactations oft the subsection of lines at her forefinger joint, where the grooves turns anaglyptan like the pink kitty kamaboko, still at where her shoulder jammed on an office wall. écorché with the pulled-in sag of seuratesque tights, picking the aurous spangles of a bo peep staff, emending the slow melting of opalescent green of hillock, at where they left their tails behind them. a shearing n impression she espies, as being worn under her shoes, from the board lasted fleece footbed. in his stare,

a tensing of arriving legs, leaning to an extraction of the button-up shirt, from the cubic drawer front. as the cocomonomamani is rolled out, with its button handle, like wearing white blouses on the spinner. at a pfffttt of her nylon on the seat, turning her popliteal fossa toward a pileus, left after he had gone. he taking her fold-over booties, before dislodging the smaller-sized blouse with a kind of exuberance. not reducible to getting her unassimilatory shrug. in an inelaborate silence, as she goes to where his arms were drawn away, pressing her commend of his salined bagely lump. still prodding the carmine, to a before lip broadening, cunégondel corners turned at, at the dyed substantiality of her plicaes' impingement

---

ma tei gow, Chinese water chestnut cake, that appears marbled

noppera-bō, a faceless ghost in Japanese legend, sometimes impersonating someone familiar to a person, causing their facial features to disappear

kamaboko, Japanese processed seafood product made from fish puree, often pink-skinned or white

cocomonomamani, a type of woven sock made by designer Marii Kishigami, known for giving the appearance of being worn under shoes–some with special messages or patterns that can only be seen when the shoes are removed

Cunégonde, a fictional character in Voltaire's *Candide,* who is the childhood friend and later the lover and wife of the title character, after various turns using her beauty and sexuality to manipulate men

Demission

he slaps on her mein held slippers, to the sitting at the dressing table, lifted at the satinbirch interior. finding emptied of the bottles with silver gilt tops as the palpitating fans of his fingers find a tangle of reddish brown, curling before the chemo at even the dark roots. sliding the tweezer to barely touch it, to see skittish to steadied the porcelain button's transfer of a big spot dog at the bottom of a button down robed profile's cumulonimbi. beblearing the doleful posture as he bucks, the yank teeters it on to the bone spurring of his big toe. craning the slanted end to a wiry strand, peeling it in three strokes, it slides beforehand, mixing inadvertently with the transposition from the right end of his brow. with his lids drooped again, as a gradual parade on a raised finger is unexamined, bourne in the ceiling fan's motion –blurring the rosette molding, the shade of a soft-boiled egg, shelled as the leaning of a woon wah

fleurcup in clear. paused at the non slip ridges along the stem, that he figures clasped as he bends forward, sensing it is stiffer on the bottom, while from its light nap, an orangey millimeter ambles while he half-sits, unnoticing his toe knuckle capped. brushing a cachectic strand from his nosebridge as he gazes slightingly at the emptied walls, the floors bared, the moon coming in low at windows and windscreens with the blok's pill popping surgical mask, placed over the wreath of grey hydrangea twig, aslant, ungingerly dismounting near the hardwood. the room's quiet is creaked by their conjointal egression from the bathroom. leaving a closed up syringe with gummy brain in liebesperlan, in their he'll-find-it notion. in white-lipped constipation, inclining face down on the high arch of the front apron, noticing his trouser risen affixedly, a tad below his knee, to find the prying an aminexil vial drops. his bà bà's shouts,

about layrite gone, his flat top blown, in their barging on a stooped hibakush working his calf back into a stillness, beside the other's uncrampedness, their frozenness keeping that way in the clumped duvet cover, pulled higher with a aperture of the safety pin dislodged, with its no coil to snag onto a star willow saddle's felt cantle. he dreams of being in a kind of wind, which sounds lesser like snow coming then the waved about of a flag towel's segregating crush of sighs. outside, the snow stopped falling on the poking of his mitts through the

elasticized reinforced cuffs of the grey coat to open its adjustable tunnel hood.
swooshes against the loops and attritions in the row of tv aerials he goes under.
lying in the drift, still hearing their calls for him under the viet big band song's
repeated couplets. not making out the first half, while the *ching chu lei sing lee
tai chi yah* refers to fantastical pearls. calipering, with liking the begun freezed
sensations at his toetips, the snow pocking with seam sealed serous demilunes

---

mein, face (Cantonese)

woon wah, an expression said of guys who are not serious, getting a new girlfriend
often. The phrase can also be applied to a movie theatre that changes movies often

hibakusha, refers to the surviving victims of the atomic bombings of Hiroshima
and Nagasaki

bà bà, dad

layrite, a very rich men's hair substance that holds like a wax, and that helps in
creating high pomps, slick backs, flat-tops, spikes, etc.

ching chu lei sing lee tai chi yah, refers to the mystery and grandeur of pearls.
The line appears in French-Vietnamese producer Onra's tune, an anthem that
involves deconstruction of oriental sounds

See Sweeps

reaching the piling of new tabloids, returning to the stare arching along with its saccadic pursuit in the direction of the oily swells' numberless impelling rags of foam with some beards of matted feathers, harboring the wee otter's hind feet, broadly flattened in propulsion, in the fitting against the beached sea turtle's runnel, to the fencing page's causerie of antitussive.

it patching the cup hilt rapier by the left-handed gauntlet cuff, scuffled atop the empire lampshade, two-toned with his phlegm mass in chestnut honey or snow-wet knots in his razored rain maker cut.

practicing the flashing head moil, while his throat's feeling of the sinimay liniment is like it had been distressed with a broken branch.

hardly forming the whistle of the usb memory-chip-bearing hand, the crimson clé frozed on its way beside the incomplete-in-one-dish of hot and sour shirataki, nearly finished that was suddenly laggered toward the decades' worth of construction-paper chains, thankfully smothering an other.

slumping with a cough and the nothing to blow his nose on, with a propping of his scored bridge on the romanian witch's silk gazar dress, holding out the removable press-stud fastening slip, to like the slight plexiform neurofibroma extending up a boy's thigh posteriorly. snivelling as he heads to the fitted unit off the kitchen.

the light getting to the calmly blowned fadedness in the evenly spaced images pasted on paper-doily snowflakes.

he grasps the full white goat roll to void, while his low murmuraton to get the baijiu, meets with the lotusy stuffed with glutinous heard, with seeing his form slide in to the corner with a quieted ruffle of book page.

closing his eyes as much as they could go, with a cajolery of black glovedness removed, while actually noticing the half of the tortoise shell headband, he wedges in the polythene flatus of the heater.

as he ruffles his hair octuply with his right hand and again with the left passing off the I have enough on my hands with all those pastries.

stretching his neck, he glances along the airing-cupboard and at the latchings of the rear of his head vivacedly the way the shih tzu does.

the inerrancies he urges from the wheals of the wig strands from his shoulderblade, while momentarily his face seems puffed, latticed with the ephemeral marks of rest.

in stroking his hair from the edges of the My Princess Boy cover and the trulation of its toddled pink tiara, in dropping his head softly, his ears folding in the oversized clip on geo discs.

lugging the newsprint to the gei-no-kai, with its untowering of political figure fending off a scandal, as the small parsonage lugs pendencies of faithlessness to the ground

---

shirataki, very low carbohydrate, low calorie, thin, translucent, gelatinous, traditional Japanese

baijiu, "hot liquor," a clear drink normally drunk in China, made from distilled sorghum. It has a distinct pungent scent and taste due to its high alcohol content that can exceed 70 per cent ABV

gei-no-kai, the scandalous goings-on of figures in the public eye in Japanese tabloids

Acknowledgements

"Summitting," "Craft," and "The Sorry For" appeared in http://gutlit.com/20Il. Versions of "Rime," "Red Riding Hood," "Avidity," "At the Plaza," "Dynamic Stability," "Oh Her Toes," "Costime," and "Syzygy" appeared in *grain*'s Winter 2011 issue. "Thrall" was in *Dinosaur Porn, 2010*. "On Her Toes" was included in *NōD Magazine* 2010. "At Twelve," "Nuptial Rites," and "Ocean Dome" were featured in 2010's http://www.ditchpoetry.com/louisebak.htm, while "Dim Sum" was in *Misunderstandings Magazine,* 2009. "Service Stare" was in *The New Chief Tongue 9,* 2009. "Guessable" appeared both in Toronto's *Literal World* and in http://houseofpomegranates.com/?p=664 in 2009. "Come Around" was developed from a poetry-video collaboration with Garine Torossian in 2008. "Rock 'n' Roll" appeared in *Descant*'s Margins and Borders issue in 2008, while "Alaya" was in *NōD Magazine*'s fall 2006. "Craft" was included in *Kiss Machine 8,* 2005 and in *Future Welcome: The Moosehead Anthology X* (DC Books, 2005). "Rock 'n' Roll," "Alaya," and "Dim Sum" were in *New American Writing* #23, 2005. "Rock 'n' Roll" and "Alaya" were also in *fhole 4* May 2005. "Craft" and "Close Up" appeared in *fhole 5* August 2005. An earlier version of "Alaya," was anthologized within the *Criminal's Cabinet: An Anthology of Poetry and Fiction* (nthposition press, 2004). "Dim Sum" and "The Call," appeared in *Montgomery Cliff,* 2004, while "Alaya" and "Rock 'n' Roll" were posted in nthposition.com, Spring 2002. "Rock 'n' Roll" was also in *Island 89,* Autumn 2002.

Many thanks to the Canada Council for the Arts, the Banff Centre for the Arts and Jason Camlot for his faith and wise readings of this collection. Thanks also to Winnie Truong for extending her drawings: *Nice Day for a Sulk* and *Bear Arms* to *Syzygy*. I'm grateful the author's photograph was taken in Andrea Johnson's atelier by Maylynn Quan.

Thanks also to Kemeny Babineau, Cameron Bailey, John Barlow, Daniel Bradley, Roland Brener, Tom Dean, Nancy Dembowski, Christopher Dewdney, Brian Fawcett, Rafi Ghanghounian, Greg Hollingshead, Mike Hoolboom, Sebastian Horsley, William Huffman, Eli Langer, Henry Jackman, Katrien Jacobs, Edward Kay, Liam Lacey, Niels Lomholt, Istvan Kantor, David Keyes,

Sylvia Legris, Keith Lock, Viktor Mitic, Philip Maglieri, Monte McMurchy, Philip Monk, Shai Ohayon, Coman Poon, David Salazar, Russell Smith, Susan Swan, Todd Swift, Vincent Tangredi, Tobaron Waxman, Steve Venright and Craig Yoe.

I'm grateful, as always, to my gracious mother, Jeanne Bak.

 Louise Bak is a writer and artist living in Toronto. She is the author of *Tulpa* (Coach House Books), *Gingko Kitchen* (Coach House Books) and *emeighty* (Letters). She's gained widespread attention as the co-host of Sex City, Toronto's only radio show focused on intersections between sexuality and culture. Her performance work has appeared in numerous galleries, festivals and video collaborations, including *Partial Selves, Crimes of the Heart* and *The Sister and the Priest*. She co-wrote a feature film called *The Ache*. She also hosts a salon series called The Box, which encourages communication across literary, artistic borders http://www.boxsalon.com/.